Introducing the Language of the News

Introducing the Language of the News is a comprehensive introduction to the language of news reporting. Assuming no prior knowledge of linguistics, the book provides an accessible analysis of the processes that produce news language, and discusses how different linguistic choices promote different interpretations of news texts.

Key features include:

- comprehensive coverage of both print and online news, including news design and layout, story structure, the role of headlines and leads, style, grammar and vocabulary
- a range of contemporary examples in the international press, from the 2012 Olympics, to political events in China and the Iraq War
- chapter summaries, activities, sample analyses and commentaries, enabling students to undertake their own analyses of news texts
- a companion website with extra activities, further readings and web links, which can be found at www.routledge.com/cw/busa.

Written by an experienced researcher and teacher, this book is essential reading for students studying English language and linguistics, media and communication studies, and journalism.

M. Grazia Busà is Associate Professor of English Linguistics at the University of Padova, Italy.

Introducing the Language of the News

A student's guide

M. Grazia Busà

LONDON AND NEW YORK

First published 2014
by Routledge
2 Park Square, Milton Park, Abingdon, Oxon OX14 4RN

Simultaneously published in the USA and Canada
by Routledge
711 Third Avenue, New York, NY 10017

Routledge is an imprint of the Taylor & Francis Group, an informa business

British Library Cataloguing in Publication Data
A catalogue record for this book is available from the British Library

Library of Congress Cataloging in Publication Data
Busà, Maria Grazia.
Introducing the language of the news / Maria Grazia Busà.
pages cm.
Includes bibliographical references.
1. Mass media and language. 2. Broadcast journalism--Language.
3. Newspapers--Language. 4. Discourse analysis--Social aspects. I. Title.
P96.L34B87 2013
070.101'4--dc23
2013006025

ISBN: 978-0-415-63729-9 (hbk)
ISBN: 978-0-415-63730-5 (pbk)
ISBN: 978-0-203-79706-8 (pbk)

Typeset in Sabon
by Saxon Graphics Ltd, Derby

Printed and bound in Great Britain by
TJ International Ltd, Padstow, Cornwall

Contents

Figures

Preface

This book is about the English of the news. It focuses on a set of linguistic features and analytical approaches that I, as a teacher of English Linguistics to students of communication, believe are useful to students with an interest in understanding and producing news. It offers an account of the processes that produce media language, explores the role of audiences in framing news texts, and explains how different linguistic choices promote different interpretations of news texts. It also addresses the changes that are taking place with the advent of online journalism and the new media.

Whether we are news junkies or low-information people, we are surrounded by news. Thanks to the news, we can be updated on what is happening all over the globe. We can obtain information on local, national and international current affairs, politics, finance and business, often packaged with a healthy dose of shopping advice, sport, showbiz, entertainment, science, technology, cuisine, holidays, lifestyle, fashion and celebrities' lives. Reading, watching or listening to the news fulfils our desire and our civic duty to understand what is going on around us; it increases our knowledge about the world and lets us form our own opinions and ideas of current affairs. It also provides us with topics for discussion during social or professional events.

The news comes to us in a number of formats. The oldest tool for delivering it is, of course, the newspaper. The two other traditional media are the television and the radio. These three are probably still considered the most trusted news sources, although they are currently facing harsh competition from the more recent Internet and wireless information technology. In fact, the Internet has become the largest and most widespread source of news production and consumption, with thousands of newspapers from every corner of the world available online – many at no cost, some requiring a nominal fee for full access. Portable electronic devices, such as smart phones and tablets, have become ubiquitous and are boosting people's ability to access and read news round the clock.

The easy accessibility of information from distant corners of the globe for a readership of unprecedented size makes this a golden age for news. News organizations are competing for larger audience shares and advertising revenues, and as part of this process, news is presented in many forms, ranging from factual reporting of events to sensational entertainment.

In news-making, nothing is left to chance. Every aspect of a news story – topic relevance, text size, ordering of events, number of details, level of formality, visual structure of the text – is carefully planned, and the choice made depends on both the communicative goal being pursued and the sociocultural values that are assumed to be shared with the audience.

Understanding the news requires understanding of the complexity of the process of news creation, of the relationship between the news author and the news consumer, and of how news is delivered to its audience.

Because of its key role as a language of international communication, English is increasingly used as the language of the news; it allows information to flow openly and regional voices to be heard internationally. In Asia, for example, the use of English in the media industry is being promoted officially, as it is deemed essential to exchange information internationally and to face the present-day challenges of social and economic developments.

This book is about the language of the news, the driving forces behind it, and the processes of production and consumption of the news in English. It focuses on print news, but examines aspects of online news too. There is, in fact, a conceptual continuity between the print and the online newspapers: despite many differences between print and the electronic media, online news services adopt a 'newspaper metaphor' as a basis for delivering news content in a form familiar to their readers. This metaphor accounts for many of the similarities between print and online news, and serves as an introduction to reading online news. In addition, online journalism shares with traditional journalism a code of ethics, as well as approaches, methods and practices.

This book begins by reviewing some basic concepts about language in texts (Introduction). It then provides an account of the socio-economic factors framing news (Chapter 1) and examines how news is shaped by factors such as timing, location, audience, and technology (Chapter 2), before discussing how news stories are created through reworking information from a number of sources (Chapter 3). Finally, it analyses the semiotic and linguistic resources that can be used to present information in a newspaper and in the news story: from page design and layout (Chapter 4), via article structure and characteristics (Chapters 5 and 6) to choices of style, grammatical constructions and lexicon (Chapters 7 to 9).

This book is meant to be of use to practitioners in English linguistics and communication studies, especially to students, teachers and researchers active in an EFL/ESL context.

Acknowledgements

I owe a great debt of gratitude to Sara Gesuato and Andrea Casotto for their valuable suggestions and support. I also wish to thank Dr Sue Norton and two anonymous reviewers for helpful advice.

The material below has been reproduced with kind permission of the copyright holders. Every effort has been made to obtain permission, and any omissions brought to my attention will be remedied at the earliest opportunity.

Front page of the *Independent*, UK, August 13, 2012
Front page of the *China Daily*, China, August 13, 2012
Front page of the *Gulf News*, United Arab Emirates, August 13, 2012
Front page of the *Global Times*, China, August 13, 2012
Front page of the *Boston Herald*, US, August 14, 2012
Front page of the *Daily News*, US, August 14, 2012
'China's Last Emperor's House Demolished', www.chinadaily.com.cn, August 15, 2012
'Airstrike May Have Killed Saddam', www.msnbc.msn.com, April 8, 2003
'Man Allegedly Tries to Put Wife in Oven', Associated Press, November 30, 2006
Front page of the *Daily Telegraph*, UK, October 24, 2012
Front page of the *Guardian*, UK, October 13, 2012
Front page of the *Daily Mirror*, UK, October 6, 2012
Page 18 of the *Boston Herald*, November 1, 2012
'Body Found in Burning Castro Valley Home', www.sfgate.com, October 18, 2012
'Wilson High School Student, 17, and Man, 18, Sold Ecstasy To Undercover Detective, Police Say', readingeagle.com, May 14, 2009
'Anguish in the Ruins of Mutanabi Street', Washington Post Foreign Service, March 10, 2007
'Crash Victim "An Aspiring Model"', Press Association, UK, September 17, 2012
'Suspicious Wives Master the Art of High-Tech Spying', www.dailymail.co.uk, May 24, 2010
'Health Food? Try the Dog's Dinner. Pet Meat Has Less Fat Than Big Mac', *The Sunday Times*, UK, March 26, 2006.
'Moment of Vandalism May Lead to a Lifetime in Prison', *The Times*, UK, March 13, 2007

'Cancelled Flights and Baggage Chaos Mar Terminal 5 Opening', www.thetimes.co.uk, March 27, 2008
'Man Arrested NINE Years After Air Hostess, 19, Was Killed in Car Crash on M25', www.dailymail.co.uk, November 11, 2012
'In Ghana's Witch Camps, The Accused Are Never Safe', *Los Angeles Times*, September 9, 2012
'Mexico's Newest Icon: 22-Year-Old Miss Universe', Associated Press, August 24, 2010
'Hurricane Sandy Could Bring Snow, Driving Rain to the New York City Area', www.nydailynews.com, October 25, 2012
'Mysterious Woman Flanking N.K. Leader Highly Likely to be His Wife: Gov't Source', english.yonhapnews.co.kr, July 15, 2012
'Visit by President Obama Causes Traffic Headaches in Los Angeles', www.swrnn.com, August 17, 2010
'World Agenda: "Prince Jean" and the Court of King Sarko', www.thetimes.co.uk, October 20, 2009
Page 22 of *The Times*, UK, February 26, 2008
'Bus Stop Killer's Link to Milly', the *Daily Telegraph*, UK, February 26, 2008
Front page of the *Sun*, UK, February 26, 2008

Introduction

Language and texts

This is an introduction to the notion of linguistic variation. It explains how the English language varies according to such factors as social occasion, purpose, audience, and communication medium. The notions of *genre* and *register* are discussed and exemplified with a number of texts that differ in their levels of linguistic formality and use of colloquial and/or slang expressions.

Journalists may not know linguistics theory, but it is their ability to work with language that sets them apart. As part of their practice, they collect information, select what is significant, provide background and context for it, and present it to their audience. Journalists make use of engaging language and fluid prose to create powerful stories that have import, impact, and elements of exclusivity and uniqueness. As this book will show, in journalists' stories, linguistic choices may help to provide a slant on the issue at hand: that is, to favour the representation of one viewpoint over another. This introduction establishes some key concepts about language that will be useful as we work through the topics discussed later in the book.

Linguistic competence

At the root of speakers' ability to function in a linguistic community is their communicative and linguistic **competence**. By this we mean their tacit knowledge of a language and ability to use it in ways that are appropriate to different social situations. It also refers to speakers' ability to associate language with extra-linguistic characteristics that define his/her own identity – such as age, sex, social class, level of education and regional background – or reveal his/her personality and attitude – such as happiness, sadness, enthusiasm, agreement, disappointment.

In linguistics, the range of linguistic choices or styles that speakers can control as part of their linguistic competence is referred to as **register repertoire**: that is, variations in language use. For example, individuals will use a more colloquial vocabulary when speaking to children or friends than when addressing doctors; they will use more formal language when writing to a school principal than when writing their diaries; they will use a more professional tone at work than they do at home.

In different linguistic communities, different **rules of language use** may apply. This means that discourse practices, framing oral and written language behaviour, vary from culture to culture, depending on culture-specific views about events and people. Thus, culture-specific practices govern such behaviours as greeting, thanking, apologizing, speaking in public, knowing when it is socially appropriate to talk and when not, when it is appropriate to use formal or informal language, etc. Culture-specific practices also determine which forms of address to use when speaking or writing to people, such as whether names should be preceded by titles or not. For example, the United States has long been considered an informal culture. People tend to use informal codes of conduct, wear informal clothing, and avoid using titles and honorifics. In addition, most people will quickly switch to the use of first names when meeting strangers. The generalized use of the greeting *Hi* reflects the informality of American culture. But for people from cultures that place a higher value on formality, as most Latin American, European and Asian societies do, the informality of Americans may be a source of confusion, misunderstanding and embarrassment.

People within a linguistic community will generally be able to recognize that within the context of different kinds of social activities, different types of oral and written discourse are appropriate, characterized by specific linguistic and structural features, as well as topics and communicative purposes. This too is part of speakers' linguistic competence. For example, lectures, talks, poems, plays, novels, news reports and conversations have characteristics of their own which make them different from any other kind of discourse.

These oral and written texts, used conventionally in connection with certain social activities, are called **genres**. The texts below can be identified as examples of three different communicative genres.

1 Today, I was upset over a recent break-up. It showed while I was at work, and I made a customer sad just by looking blue. She complained to my manager. I got written up for being so depressed that I got a customer depressed too.

(entry from www.fmylife.com)

2 Communication involves the transmission and reception of meaning at multiple levels. It is only by taking into account all the elements combining and integrating in the communication process, that effective communication can be taught.

(adapted from an academic paper by M.G. Busà)

3 Buzzy Bee is not like other bees. Other bees find their honey only during the day. Buzzy Bee finds honey during the night. Night lilies taste yummy. 'Hmm, this flower isn't bad', says the bee. 'Uh oh. Where am I?'

(adapted from: www.magickeys.com/books/beenight/index.html)

Text 1 is an anecdote from a person's life; 2 is an excerpt from an academic paper; and 3 is the beginning of a children's story. Each presents characteristics that distinguish it from the other two. In 1, the choice of the topic, the presence of short juxtaposed sentences, the use of colloquial words (*break-up*, meaning 'termination'; *looking blue*, meaning 'being disheartened'; *got written up*, meaning 'got a demerit') make the text rather informal and conversational, appropriate to a simple recounting of personal events. In Text 2 the topic, the use of long and complex sentences, the presence of formal words, mostly of Latin origin (*communication, involves, transmission, reception, multiple, combining, integrating, effective*), identify this as an academic text, targeting linguistics or communication scholars. Finally, in Text 3 the topic, the simple syntactic structures, alliterative language (*Buzzy Bee*) and child-oriented lexicon (*yummy* meaning 'good') characterize the text as a children's story, which needs to be simple to be understood and enjoyed by its audience.

Understanding that texts can be recognized by their linguistic characteristics is essential to the interpretation of news texts. The following section reviews another important characteristic of discourse: that is, linguistic variation.

Variation in language

As we have seen in the preceding section, all speakers control a range of linguistic choices or styles, referred to as **registers**, which they can use to make their language appropriate to the situation they are in. A number of variables combine to define the situation in which speakers use language and shape the linguistic register they use.

Discourse topic and participants' background

The first two variables affecting register concern the extent to which the information presented in the text is shared, or assumed to be shared, with the audience. The first variable is **topic**. Text topics can range from highly specialized and/or technical – e.g., a scientific paper or a description of a chemical substance – to everyday and conversational – e.g. gossiping or talking about shopping. The second variable is the **participants** involved in the discourse. These vary in their degree of familiarity with the topic at hand: they may be experts in the field (e.g., scientists, surgeons, etc.) or have basic knowledge of the topic, such as the readers of a newspaper article.

Together the discourse topic and participants determine the type of language used in the text (everyday, technical, jargon, slang), as well as the amount of information that is taken for granted or explained. For example, a text written for specialists will use a large number of technical terms and fewer explanations, because the writer will assume that that information is known by the audience; a text written for the layperson will contain fewer technical terms and more explanations, as the writer will assume that much of the information is not known by the audience.

The two texts below exemplify these differences:

1 An example of a supercooled liquid can be made by heating solid sodium acetate trihydrate ($NaCH_3CO_2$ 3 H_2O). When this solid melts, the sodium acetate dissolves in the water that was trapped in the crystal to form a solution. When the solution cools to room temperature, it solidifies.

(chemed.chem.purdue.edu/genchem/topicreview/bp/ch14/melting.php)

2 In physics, nuclear fusion (a thermonuclear reaction) is a process in which two nuclei join to form a larger nucleus, thereby giving off energy. Nuclear fusion is the energy source that causes stars to 'shine', and hydrogen bombs to explode.

(allwebhunt.com/dir-wiki.cfm/nuclear_fusion)

Both texts provide an explanation of scientific phenomena. However, the first text is written by a scientist for students of physics; it is characterized by a highly technical lexicon and includes formulas and long compounds for which no explanation is provided, as this terminology is assumed to be known by the students. The second explains the phenomenon of nuclear fusion to the general public: it is written with simple words, limiting the use of technical terms to familiar ones (e.g., *thermonuclear reaction*, *nucleus*), and making reference to phenomena that are well known to an audience of non-experts (i.e., *shining stars* and *exploding bombs*).

Relationship with the audience

A third variable affecting texts relates to the type of **relationship** existing, presumed or invoked between the discourse participants. This can vary according to: status (ranging from unequal, as in the case of a boss and an employee, to equal, as between friends); affective involvement (which can be high with friends/family members, or low with business clients); contact (ranging from frequent to occasional). The relationship between participants determines the speaker's (or writer's) linguistic choices, and these choices signal the type of relationship the speaker (or writer) wants to establish with the listener (or reader). The use of formal language implies distance; less formal language conveys or establishes a sense of proximity, community and friendliness with the audience.

The following two excerpts tell the same story, but with different degrees of formality.

1 Hey, just signed up a few minutes ago! I'm Karen, and the things happening in my life right now are just awesome. I'm finishing up Business School. I only have two weeks left!!!! I'm soooo stoked about that, I can't stand my job at the pastry shop any more. I so want something new and different! But I'm gonna tell you guys all kinds of cool and interesting stuff! Take it easy!

(invented example)

2 Ladies and Gentlemen, let me introduce myself. I'm Karen Jones, and my life is about to change a great deal. I will be finishing Business School in two weeks. I am very excited about that. This also means that I'll be changing my old job at the local pastry shop. It'll be a good change and a challenging opportunity. I'll be sharing all the details of this interesting experience in this forum. Thank you and have a good day.

(rewritten from the text above)

The first text, written with an informal language and tone, is characterized by expressions that are typical of spoken language (*Hey, Take it easy, you guys*); incomplete sentences (lack of subject in the first sentence); use of slang words (*I'm stoked,* i.e., I'm excited); spellings that mimic emphasis in speech (*soooo*) or reflect casual pronunciation (*gonna*); constructions that would be considered ungrammatical in traditional prescriptive grammars but are frequently heard in the speech of young people *(I so want*). The second text is characterized by the use of formulae typically used in formal situations (i.e., *Ladies and Gentlemen*; *I'm Karen Jones*; *Thank you and have a good day*), the use of complete sentences (no subjects or verbs missing), and no slang. While the first text would be appropriate if addressed to young people, fellow students or the like, the second text would be more appropriately targeted to adults or an unfamiliar audience.

Purpose

Another variable affecting the language of texts relates to the **purpose** for which they are written. The purpose is the goal one aims to attain when producing a text. For example, the purpose of a textbook or a lecture is to help students to learn. The purpose of advertisements is to persuade people to buy. The purpose of many documentaries is to inform. The purpose of comics or a joke is to make people laugh, or at least chuckle. In each case, the purpose of the text will influence the way in which it is composed. Thus, a descriptive passage will contain language that will help the reader imagine how something (or someone) looks, sounds, smells, tastes or feels. In contrast, the information in an instructional booklet will be aimed at explaining how something works.

In fact, purpose, audience and situation are very closely linked. This is because the purpose of a text often involves communicating with a particular audience. A story written with the purpose of making children laugh will need an audience of children, and to succeed in this purpose the writer needs a good understanding of the situation: i.e., what is likely to interest children and move them to laughter.

Spoken and written language

The characteristics of a text depend also on the way it is delivered. A preliminary distinction is that between spoken and written texts. In general, **spoken language** is spontaneous, whereas **written language** is planned. Spoken language is characterized by hesitations, interruptions, false starts, repetitions, omissions, a large use of pronouns, the use of colloquial and informal expressions, simple grammatical structures. Conversely, written language tends to be more structured, with well-formed and articulated sentences, and makes use of more formal lexicon and more complex constructions. The example below is a transcript from an actual conversation between a bank clerk (**B**) and a customer (**C**). The text shows many typical features of spoken language: hesitations (*uh*, *hm*); pauses (...); false starts (line 4, *you haven't ... you're not ...*) rephrased expressions (line 6, *from the bank to ... uhh: ... uhh: to a ... the ... an account)*, incomplete sentences (lines 10–12, *so that's why* ...). The language of this text can be contrasted with that of the examples above, which were all intended to be written texts.

B: Can I help you?
C: Uh: yes, I would like to have some information, hm ... to find out what I need to do to get a mortgage ... I haven't got an account in here.
B: You haven't ... you're not an investor with us?
C: Hmmm, no, but I got some money in the bank so I will be able to transfer the money from the bank to ... uhh: ... uhh: to a ... the ... an account.
B: You've seen a property, then.
C: Hmmm ... I saw something, but I- I saw a couple of places that ... uh ... but ... I- I don't know ... uh ... if I find a place what I have to do ... so that's why ...

(from a conversation in a bank recorded by M.G. Busà)

Texts can also be written to be spoken, as in the case of political speeches, TV shows, radio newscasts and play scripts. Such texts are characterized by well-constructed sentence and discourse structures, with few hesitations, omissions or repetitions. As a result they appear to be planned texts, even though they present features that are typically associated with spoken language, such as the use of contracted forms and colloquial expressions, and dialogues. In the next example below, a few characteristics suggest that the speaker may be following a written text: the choice of educated rather than colloquial words; the presence of long and complex sentence structures; the lack of interruptions and/or repetitions; and the fact that it is a monologue addressed to an audience.

> Mr Chairman, Your Excellency, Honourable Ministers of State, Distinguished Delegates, Ladies and Gentlemen, On behalf of all civil society organizations working in peace and security in Ghana, I wish to extend a warm welcome to you all to Ghana and to this conference […].[1]

In other cases, written language can mimic spoken language, as often occurs in chats, texting, blogs, emails, etc., which are characterized by very little planning. Written language that mimics spoken language can also be used by writers who wish to create a 'friendly', informal relationship with their readers, e.g., in popular magazines, newspapers, websites, forums. Below is an example of a written text that imitates speech (taken from a web poll on the popular singer Justin Bieber).

> omigod do u like like so totally luv justin bieber!? Or do think hes not even worth thinking about?
>
> (entry from: www.quibblo.com)

The type of transmission **medium** used to deliver it also affects the characteristics of the text. For example, there are considerable differences between texts written to be read on paper and those intended for reading off the computer screen. The first difference concerns the layout. In texts for print, there is a tendency to minimize the empty space on the page; hence print pages typically contain a lot of text, and white space on the page is reduced. In texts for the screen, on the other hand, fonts are preferred that allow for extra space between characters (Verdana may be preferred to Times New Roman, for example), and lines and formats are chosen that leave a lot of white space on the page. These choices are aimed at easing the reading process, which appears to be slower and more fatiguing when done from a screen than from paper. A second difference concerns the content: the transient nature of the digital format makes electronic texts easier to modify than texts written for paper, which instead become fixed once they have been printed. This may result in electronic texts being revised more often than print texts, which may affect the quality of online versus print publications: being more permanent, the latter tend to be checked more often than the former, and thus can be more accurate.

Distinguishing between formal and informal English

We have seen that different social situations call for different linguistic choices. And attention has been drawn to the differences between spoken and written language – particularly the fact that the latter typically uses more formal language.

The difference between formal and informal language is not always clear-cut, though, and it is more appropriate to talk about a continuum of variation between the two. But what is it that makes language formal or informal? Some of the features distinguishing formal from informal English are summarized below.

The more informal a text is, the more it will use:

- colloquial words and expressions (*kids*, *guy*, *awesome*, *a lot*) and phrasal verbs (*get up*, *go out*, *run down*, *look into*);
- contracted forms (*can't*, *won't*, *shouldn't*, *ain't*);
- verb structures rather than noun structures, human subjects over inanimate subjects (*John solved the problem* (informal) vs. *John's solution of the problem* (formal));
- active verbs rather than passive verbs (*They finished their job* (informal) vs. *Their job was finished* (formal));
- short sentences and a preference for co-ordination (i.e., clauses linked with conjunctions such as *and*, *or*, *but*) over subordination (i.e., clauses linked with conjunctions such as *although*, *as if*, *as much as*, *even if*, *provided that*, etc.). For example: *She finished the job and went home* (informal) vs. *After finishing the job, she went home* (formal).

The more formal a text is the more it will use:

- words of French or Latin origin (*investigate*, *accommodate*, *inspect*);
- non-contracted forms (*do not*, *will not*, *should not*, etc.);
- inanimate nouns as subjects of a sentence (*The question was* ... (compare to less formal *he wondered* ...));
- passive verbs in preference to active verbs (*He was asked* (formal) vs. *They asked him* (informal));
- verbal nouns – that is, nouns created from verbs. Examples: *arrive* → *arrival*; *predict* → *prediction*; *write* → *writing*. For example: *I think of you* → *The thought of you.*

- long sentences, with a preference for subordination over co-ordination (see above). Example: *The government was obliged to take fiscal measures to reduce the likelihood of a surge in consumer spending led by cheaper imports.*

The examples in (1) and (2) show sentences having the same meaning but differing in formality level.

1 **Formal:** Because of the inclement climatic conditions, the President was obliged to return earlier than scheduled.
  Informal: The weather was bad and the president had to go back sooner than he'd planned.
2 **Formal:** Please await instructions before dispatching items.
  Informal: Don't send anything off until I tell you to do so.

A note on varieties of English around the world

To conclude, this introduction must briefly mention the variation in the English language as it is used around the world. For more on this topic, see the Further Reading section below.

Any consideration of English as one of the languages of international communication worldwide must start from the notion of what commonly goes under the name of 'English'. In fact, English comprises a variety of different 'Englishes', all showing profound modifications depending on the geographical location were they are spoken. These modifications concern all aspects of the language, though they are probably often more noticeable at the level of vocabulary and pronunciation. They are the result of linguistic adaptation to the evolving needs of global communication. This process of adaptation helps to increase the flexibility of the English language as well as its suitability for use by speakers of very diverse linguistic and cultural backgrounds. At the same time, however, varieties of English that are heavily 'coloured' by a local language may be difficult to understand for people who are not familiar with them. In news stories written in English in different parts of the world, it may not be uncommon to find that words being used to talk about a specific cultural aspect or political situation can only be understood by people who know the language and culture of the country where the news was published. Chapter 9 provides some of these examples. Being aware that present-day English can appear and be used in many forms, particularly on the Internet, is a necessary condition for approaching English as the international language of the news.

Students' activities

Activity 1

Look at the sentences below and decide if they are written in formal or informal language. Think of a plausible context in which they might occur. Explain how the situation affects the language.

Excuse me, is the manager in his office? I have an appointment.
No eating or drinking here!
Hey, how about dinner?
They've got all the info.
A great deal of crime goes unreported
Every effort is being made to obtain compensation.
The original copy was recently destroyed.
She's given us loads to do!!

Activity 2

Look at the following excerpts. Underline all the words that belong to informal/slang registers. Using the dictionary, search for the meanings of the words and find more formal equivalents.

1 Actor Jason London was dazed, confused and worse for the wear Sunday night after being arrested for assault and disorderly conduct at a bar in Scottsdale, Ariz. He allegedly sneezed on and then slugged a fellow patron.

(www.thehollywoodgossip.com, Jan. 29, 2013)

2 Following a long transcontinental flight, Channing Tatum strolled off of an airplane at JFK International Airport in New York City yesterday.

The 'Magic Mike' stud looked a bit worn out as he carried his bag through the busy terminal upon his arrival from Los Angeles.

(celebrity-gossip.net, Jan. 31, 2013)

3 Fans of the HBO hit 'Entourage' now have even more to look forward to, as a big screen deal for the show was green lighted by Warner Bros.

The series ended its television run in 2011 after seven years, and major changes are ahead for the characters.

(celebrity-gossip.net, Jan. 31, 2013)

4 Grabbing some grub to go, Leighton Meester stopped at Hugo's Restaurant in Los Angeles on Wednesday.

> The 'Gossip Girl' star showed off her svelte frame in a black tank top, gray cardigan, black leggings, and gray Uggs as she carried her lunch back to her car.
>
> (celebrity-gossip.net, Jan. 31, 2013)

Activity 3

Choose a passage each from a textbook, a magazine article and a print advertisement, possibly on similar or related topics, and compare them. For each text, decide:

- Who is the intended audience of the text?
- What is the goal of the text? (what is its communicative purpose? – e.g., is it written to explain, to convince, to promote?)
- How does the intended audience affect the content and presentation of the text?
- Is the language used in the text colloquial? Formal? Are there any slang words?

Explain the differences existing between the texts in relation to the differences in intended audience and communicative purpose.

Activity 4

Write an entry for one of the free diary sites that are available online (e.g., www.my-diary.org/; http://diary.com/; http://www.opendiary.com/). You may first want to look at a few examples, to get an idea of how people write online diary entries. Then, write the same story as an entry for your journal, reporting something interesting that happened to you in the last week. Do you need to make any changes to adapt your story to the journal? What changes concern the layout of the text? What changes concern the language? What changes concern the content?

Further reading

Dillon, A. 1992. 'Reading from paper versus screens: a critical review of the empirical literature', *Ergonomics* 35, 10, 1297–1326.

Dyson, M. 2004. 'How physical text layout affects reading from screen', *Behaviour and Information Technology* 23, 6, 377–93.

Eggins, S. 1994. *An Introduction to Systemic Functional Linguistics*, London, Pinter.

Hymes, D. 1972. 'Models of the interaction of language and social life', in J.J. Gumperz and D. Hymes (eds), *Directions in Sociolinguistics: The Ethnography of Communication*, New York, Holt, Rinehart & Winston.

Samovar, L.A., Porter, R.E., and McDaniel, E.R. 2009. *Communication between Cultures*, Boston MA, Wadsworth.

Schiffrin, D. 1994. *Approaches to Discourse: Language as Social Interaction*, Malden MA, Blackwell.

Seargeant, P. 2012. *Exploring World Englishes: Language in a Global Context*, London and New York, Routledge.

Chapter 1

Making news

This chapter presents an overview of the media industry, discussing in particular the factors that frame the news, such as newspaper ownership, market pressure, journalists' subdivision of roles and responsibilities in the newsroom, time deadlines, and space-on-the-page constraints. The last section discusses the impact of technology and multimedia on news production.

1.1 News as texts

What is news and what characterizes news texts? News texts are written to report information on new or current events and are relayed to a mass audience by print, broadcast or the Internet. News texts are shaped by news agencies' objectives and agendas and the kind of reception expected from the audience. Behind their creation lies a complex process involving organizational, economic and socio-political factors. This chapter explains what is involved in news creation, focusing in particular on the factors that drive the news world and affect news-making and -delivering.

1.2 Who controls the news?

An important factor affecting news and journalism is **ownership**. In the past it was often the case that newspapers' owners would use their paper to convey their own political views and interests. Today newspaper owners' interference in the editorial issues, in the form of *direct* control of the choice and content of the paper, is not as frequent – though big owners like Rupert Murdoch will still occasionally get involved in the editorial content of their papers (House of Lords Select Committee on Communications, 2008: 34). Ownership is more likely to have an *indirect* influence on the news output. For example, owners can influence the editorial contents and agenda simply by appointing the newspaper's editor. This will give owners some assurance that the editor will present news content that is in line with their viewpoint.

Another factor that affects news-making is owners' concern with short-term **profits** as opposed to medium-term investments. Owners who are less concerned with immediate profit can invest in the newspaper, and hire more journalists to devise new layouts, find new stories or present new perspectives on common stories. This will affect the quality of the paper and increase its chances of appealing to wide audiences. On the other hand, owners seeking short-term profits will cut their investments in journalism, for example by reducing the number of staff or saving on investigative reporting, with an effect on the overall practices and quality of the paper.

In recent decades large **global media organizations**, and huge management companies behind them, have taken over a number of newspapers, dramatically reducing the number of independent news suppliers. For example, in Britain eight owners dominate the national press; twenty publishers own 85% of all the regional market and 96% of the total weekly circulation. Most of the companies that own national newspapers also have large holdings in other media enterprises: in the US, eight companies control the majority of the media; in the world, six multinational companies effectively control the leading media. The media giants are looking with particular interest at the Asian market, where new media corporations are forming and linking up with the big international players.

The consolidation of news organizations in the hands of large media enterprises also affects **online news**. This is provided by a variety of sources, a major one being publishers of print newspapers, who maintain sites issuing news that is similar, in both presentation and content, to that of their printed papers. In addition, a number of mainstream media and Internet-based organizations provide content that may be either originated directly for the site or aggregated from well-established news sources. These include large TV networks, such as CNN (www.cnn.com), ABC (abc.go.com), BBC (news.bbc.co.uk), and Microsoft-owned NBC (www.nbcnews.com), that have been able to use their infrastructure and popularity to transfer their dominance from the mainstream media to the Internet and create a strong online presence. Other Internet corporations, such as AOL Inc. (www.aol.com), Google (news.google.com), Yahoo! (news.yahoo.com), have leveraged their popularity as search engines to expand into the world of news providers. With their ubiquitous online presence, they all can attract huge international audiences and boost profits with advertising revenues.

One of the consequences of newspaper acquisitions by large corporations is that news creation is only one of many fields in which they operate, and these are companies whose main, or only, purpose is profit. The concentration of media ownership in the hands of a few conglomerates also poses the risk of a lack of competition and diversity between different suppliers. When only a few companies represent the interests of a minority elite controlling the public airwaves, there is a higher chance that main news sites might present biased views on the events they report. On the other hand, the coexistence of different ownerships helps to ensure that a variety of views and interests are represented in the press.

In addition to a press dominated by big monopolies and organizations, all countries have an 'alternative' press, owned by smaller organizations, which often have strong political, religious or ethnic affiliations. This kind of press often presents a valid alternative to mainstream local and national press, but its circulation tends to be limited and its impact on the national debate only marginal.

Similarly, on the Internet, news is also available on websites maintained by small organizations or individual 'bloggers' who comment on the news, provide links, and occasionally even report stories. Blogging has in fact had an increasing influence on news reporting, and most online papers have included a 'Blogs' section in their daily editions.

Whatever the news provider, it is important to emphasize that, even if news was once the exclusive domain of professional journalists, it is now being delivered by a number of different actors, who may vary in competence and professional background, but all contribute to the ongoing transformation of the world of the news. The proliferation of news providers offers a variety of sources of information for consumers of news, who can now decide to get both the mainstream and the alternative perspectives and thus form their own opinions on the reported event.

1.3 Economic factors

News agencies are very much like any other business: their aim is to generate profit. While the revenues a newspaper makes from the customers' payments at the newsstand are relatively small, the key factor in generating profit is **sales** and **circulation**: that is, the number of papers in circulation on an average day, both through subscriptions and newsstand sales. Sales and circulation are important because they determine the paper's appeal and service charge to advertisers, who are the paper's real source of profit. Newspaper publishers are therefore always striving to keep sales and circulation high, so as to attract **advertising**. When sales and circulation fail to meet advertisers' requirements, papers may have to change their market segment and modify their contents to accommodate advertisers; in the worst-case scenario, they may have to close down, or look for an alternative source of patronage.

However, newspaper readership and circulation is on the decline in most countries of the world. In part this is due to the advent of the Internet, which offers many ways to get news from a variety of sources at no cost to the user. Web- or mobile-based platforms also help to make news services ubiquitously and continuously accessible to readers through portable devices such as cell phones, tablets and games consoles. In fact, it has been shown that the use of new technologies to access news may be on the rise:

teens and adults increasingly use portable devices to go online, and this is likely to increase the importance of digital platforms for reading news. Another reason for falling newspaper readership is changing lifestyles: today's fast-paced life leaves people little time to read newspapers, so news offered in a condensed, synoptic format, through mobile devices or free papers (see below), is often more appealing to a general audience than what traditional papers provide.

On their side, advertisers now have a wider range of ways to place their ads than before, and the Internet offers the option of targeting advertising at specific audiences and at lower cost than using print. Because it is so much cheaper, advertisers are spending more on Internet advertising and less and less on print.

In response to current challenges and to boost sales and circulation, newspapers may resort to promotional techniques, including price-cutting and 'giveaways' (for example, coupons), special editions, or funny pages (the comic strip sections carried in most American newspapers). To meet the readership's expectations of both the form and content of the paper's output, newspapers may also focus more on entertainment and 'soft' (as opposed to 'hard') news: something that is part of an overall tendency towards the 'tabloidization' of news (see section 1.7 below). Finally, decisions on content may also reflect pressure from advertisers, who may want a say in the paper's output in order to guarantee a target for their ads.

Because advertising pays for most of a newspaper's costs, the final reader pays little or nothing for the newspaper. In recent years a number of free publications have appeared and have enjoyed great success, particularly among the young. Typically, such newspapers are tabloid in format (i.e., smaller-sized papers) and provide readers with a sort of news bulletin, that is, a condensed version of news on a vast array of things: local, national and international events, lifestyle, technology, media, sports, celebrities, movies and service (weather forecasts, comics, horoscope, TV-guide, movie or theatre tips, crosswords). Free newspapers have been introduced in almost every European country and in several markets in the United States, Canada, South America, Australia and Asia. The market leader newspaper, *Metro*, distributes eight million free copies daily, while other companies publish at least 22 million copies. Worldwide, at least 60 million people read these 30 million copies daily. While traditional newspapers continue losing their appeal, free newspapers are doing very well, especially among the young.

As for online news, advertising is the only source of revenues for most providers. This is because the access to the majority of online news websites is free, even though some newspapers have started charging subscription fees. In fact, the newspaper business is betting heavily on web advertising revenues to secure its survival, as visitors to Internet news sites continue to grow while print circulation and advertising swoon. With the Internet and the possibility to reach huge audiences internationally, newspapers also see an opportunity to raise their international profiles. This is particularly true for any online news publication that is written in English, because it can be read by millions of people in many countries of the world.

1.4 News as the work of many

Many people collaborate in the process of news making: reporters, editors, and managers. Editors and reporters work in the newsroom, the place where the news is created, while managers take care of the financial and administrative matters of the newspaper, as well as the workplace in general.

Reporters are briefed and assigned a story to cover by the news editor. They gather information, check it for accuracy and write the original copy (that is, the article), usually according to the newspaper's own house style. Reporters are also responsible for getting the best pictures to go with the story – they may take the pictures themselves or ask photographers to take them. After the reporter has written a story, this gets sent to the news editor for approval and then to the sub-editor for revision.

Editors run the editorial activities in the newsroom; they make decisions regarding the direction that the paper will take on any particular issue; have the final say over editorial decisions such as which stories will be given relevance in the paper, and which pictures and headlines should accompany the stories. They also review photographs, pictures, headlines and page layouts. Every day, editors hold conferences to delegate specific work to various supervisory editors (including the news editor and the picture editor) or specialized editors (political editor, finance editor, sports editor). News editors also organize daily news-gathering and writing activities, assign stories, brief reporters and instruct them on the approach to adopt, the length of the story and the deadline for its completion; lastly, they check the reporter's final copy before it is passed to the sub-editor. Together with production editors or chief subs, news editors also decide which story should be assigned prominence in a page and which should be held over. Picture editors make final decisions about the pictures to use for the stories, and how these can be cropped – based on their relevance for the story, their position and their relation to the text, bearing in mind the desired effect and the space available on the page.

Sub-editors (also sub-eds, or 'subs') work under a chief sub-editor and are responsible for ensuring that the tone, style and layout of the final copy match the publication's house style and suit the target market. They check the copy for accuracy after the news editor has seen it, and may ask the reporter for changes. They correct possible spelling or grammatical errors, and may rearrange the story to change its structure, reduce its length, and make stylistic adjustments. Sub-eds are also responsible for designing pages, laying out stories, adding headlines, bylines and figure captions.[1]

With the advent of multimedia technology, the Internet and the newspapers' presence on the web, the roles and skills required by the staff employed in the newsroom have changed. Increasingly, journalists are required to be able to multi-skill – to master skills in more than one of the various modes of journalism: print, audio, television, or online. Multi-skilling has become important for journalists, who may have to be prepared to take on the roles of writers, sub-editors, photographers and editors. This has led many to view multi-skilling as a threat to the profession of journalism, fearing that it may force journalists to let go of their specializations, and that pressure due to increased workloads may cause the overall quality of journalistic practices to fall into a decline. However, multi-skilling also gives journalists greater flexibility, a better understanding of the various different production processes, and increased control over their outputs. Moreover, by giving journalists the possibility of establishing more direct contact with the readership through the use of social media, it may also restore the trust of some readers in the newspaper.

1.5 Time deadlines and space-on-the-page constraints

An important role in the final news output is played by constraints of time and space. Of the two, **time** constraints are probably more crucial. The journalist's life is ruled by deadlines: for any single event, all effort will be vain if the story is not finished in time and so cannot make it into the paper. Time inevitably affects how much information a journalist can gather for a story – it may prevent the validation of reports or the proper checking of facts and lead journalists to publish or broadcast work that is not in a 'perfect' state. In online news, stories can be updated several times during the day, and their later versions may be more accurate than earlier ones.

Time constraints are exacerbated by staffing limitations and the imposition of multi-skilling, both due to cost-cutting. The former particularly challenge the journalist doing breaking news or investigative work; the latter requires the completion of many time-consuming technical steps. As a result, even journalists who want to strive for quality in news reporting may end up producing news that is superficial rather than comprehensive.

An example of how time may constrain reporters' ability to fact-check their stories is provided by the article in Chapter 3 on pages 44–5. Written on April 8, 2003, this reports the possible death due to an air strike of Iraq's dictator Saddam Hussein in the frantic timeline of events during the Iraqi war (2003–2011). The news, which turned out to be false, was actually posted for less than an hour in the morning edition of MSNBC news (www.msnbc.msn.com), before being replaced with a piece that contained details of the air strike and its mortal effects on the local people, but did not mention Saddam's death. In fact, Saddam Hussein was found and executed nearly three years after this article appeared.

In print news, journalists are also affected by **space-on-the-page** constraints. Because the space on the page is limited, any story is competing for that space with other stories and with advertising. This imposes limits on how much text journalists can write for any given story and requires them to condense the story information into short texts written in a concise and compact style typical of news reporting (see Chapter 5). Knowing that before it makes it to the press a story may be shortened, as a result of editorial decisions, journalists prioritise the most important information at the beginning of the story, lest the ending get lost when the editor cuts the story. The tendency to write stories with an eye to how they can be cut, if needed, has contributed to the development of the most frequently used style in news reporting, the so-called 'Inverted Pyramid' style, which will be discussed in Chapter 5.

In online news, on the other hand, the space on the page is virtually unlimited, and news topics and content need not be restricted by the number or size of the pages. Having no limits of space on the page, journalists can feel free to publish 'all the news that fits in a piece' (McAdams, 1995). Also, stories can be linked to background or detailed information, and enhanced by adding audio, pictures, videos, tables, which enable journalists to provide a more comprehensive perspective of the reported event. By creating multidimensional news, journalists can appeal to readers' different senses, as well as involving readers with different degrees of interest in the news (i.e., both the surfing reader and the one searching for detailed information). At the same time, news organizations use the unlimited space to create online papers with a large number of sections and topics. This makes the paper appealing to a wide range of readers and increases its attractiveness for advertisers.

1.6 Effects of information technology

Beyond the constraints of time and space on the page, news production is also affected by the options afforded by the technologies it exploits.

Journalism has always been inextricably linked to technology. The use of devices for gathering and transmitting information (from printing devices, to telegraphs, telephones, cameras, typewriters, etc.) has characterized journalistic developments, and has impacted on the emergence of journalistic practices and values. For example, when photography was first invented in the 1830s, it was used in journalism for its evidential value and contributed to the development of the sense of accuracy, authoritativeness and objectivity of news reports. Today, too, the continuing evolution in information and communication technology is bringing major changes to the journalist's profession and to overall news production.

In the first place, technology is changing the way reporters work. Modems and satellite phones allow multimedia material and page layouts to be transmitted from very remote sites. Specialized computer software and digital networks allow journalists to research background information on the web, compare sources, collect data in databases, analyse figures and public records with statistical software, and use email to contact and interview people. Consequently, computers are an essential tool for gathering and processing information in every phase of the news story development, giving rise to what is also known as 'computer-assisted reporting' (CAR). As a result, more data are readily available for journalists to conduct their investigations, and these can be increasingly carried out from the journalist's desk, rather than in the field.

Technology is also changing the way news is produced at an operational level. In the traditional newsroom, journalists had fixed roles in a linear news production process that started at the news desk and ended in the print or broadcast room. In recent years text- and image-processing technologies have made editing and composition easier and faster. Newspaper pages can be laid out and rearranged many times, and all the elements in the page can be repositioned or resized at will. Collaborative software allows more people to work simultaneously at news composition and editing from their on-site or off-site desks, and web-based tools allow automatic updating of all users' changes. Pictures can be cropped, edited or manipulated at any stage of the composition process. Changes to the final version can be introduced until a few minutes before the news goes to the press, goes online, or is broadcast.

The use of technology has extended deadlines for journalists, partly offsetting the pressure they are under. The fact that a story can now be edited until the last few minutes before the presses roll or it goes online allows journalists to work closer to deadline, and in fact they 'are increasingly expected to do so' (Campbell, 2004). However, working close-to-deadline is a source of tension, and not the only one, for the journalist. The workload in the newsroom has generally increased as newspapers have shown a tendency to cover more events, expand their numbers of pages and sections, and add more pictures, diagrams, plots, etc. Report updating can take place several times during news composition and editing, and broadcast and online journalists are required to produce several bulletins a day or update the newspaper's site continuously.

At the same time, multimedia technology is now accessible to non-journalistic organizations and members of the general public. This, by creating the conditions allowing anyone to produce news or contribute to news circulation, puts an end to the role of the journalist as the sole provider of news. It is not infrequent that descriptive images of a major event come from private citizens who have taken pictures of it, perhaps with their smart phone.

Multimedia technology is also changing the role of the audience, which is no longer passively consuming what is produced by the journalist, but has in fact an interactive role in contributing to news making and interpretation (for example, through emails, blogs, forums, comments, etc.). The different role of the audience, if marginal in conventional TV or print news, has dramatically changed news presentation and delivery on the Internet.

1.7 The impact of 'convergence' on the world of news

Finally, multimedia technology is contributing to blurring distinctions between originally different media forms. In the recent past, the world of media communication has been changed by what is called '**media convergence**' (or simply 'convergence'). Convergence is used to indicate the unification of all earlier media forms (print, audio, video, animation, telephone) in a single medium that can reach new and wide audiences. As Wilkinson (2003) says: 'The Internet has recently changed our favourite delivery systems – Newspapers now provide video, TV offers interactive chat, and radio has web-cams.'

Convergence has revolutionized the way news is conceived and provided. At the organizational level, convergence is represented by the concentration of media organizations in the hands of large global corporations (see section 1.2 above). This has the effect of bridging distinctions between types of news productions that were once separate, for example, print, radio and broadcast. News from the same source can now be provided to an audience in any desired form (print, video, audio, text), on any device (radio, TV, computer, portable phone, etc.) and at any time. The unification of different media formats is contributing to the 'spectacularization' (or 'tabloidization') of news reporting, in which sensationalism – as determined by the amount of audio, video and image material available to the journalist – largely determines news selection and presentation.

Convergence is also contributing to changing journalists' methods and practices – and ultimately some basic aspects of the journalistic profession. The ability to multi-skill and expertise in multimedia, which make journalists capable of producing content that is suitable to multiple formats (see section 1.4), are highly valued in news organizations and have become part of the requirements of the modern journalist, to the disadvantage of journalists with a particular specialism.

Students' activities

Activity 1

Choose a story, written in English, from a national paper. Then compare and contrast how this story is covered in different media and by different networks, illustrating the differences with specific examples.

Activity 2

Compare a news story written by the same news provider for its print edition and its online edition. Discuss the differences in the overall layout of the story, looking in particular at:

- white space in the page;
- amounts of text and visual/graphical elements in the page;
- paragraph format;
- bullets, lines and any other graphical elements in the page;
- size of characters, pictures, presence of video clips (in the online story).

Explain how the observed differences between the layout of the print text and the electronic text can be related to the different technology and medium used to deliver the texts.

Activity 3

Some of the techniques that can be used to make a story more gripping (i.e. more sensationalistic) are listed below. Search for a dramatic news story in a print or online paper, and find how some of these techniques are used. Alternatively, you may want to use the examples at the end of the list.

- **False Novelty** (presenting something as news when in fact it has been known for a long time: e.g., *Flu outbreak expected to hit this winter*);[2]
- **False Urgency** (creating a sense that things are happening or developing more quickly than they actually are, so as to add drama to the story: e.g., *The leaning tower of Pisa is collapsing*);
- **Exaggerated Risk** (reporting on a very unlikely danger without mentioning the likelihood of it actually happening, or exaggerating the consequences of a possible danger: e.g., *Hurricane Sandy to Destroy East Coast & Wall Street*);
- **Leaving Out Details** (leaving out parts of the story that might make it less exciting: e.g., *Swallowing cinnamon may cause death* – this headline does not mention that it is irritation in the lungs, possibly followed by pneumonia, that is the real cause of death).

- **Emotional Language and Imagery** (using language or images that may excite or anger people: e.g., *8 reasons why your holiday romance is doomed*).

Examples:

1 **News interview interrupted by dramatic arrest**

(news.ninemsn.com.au, January 31, 2013)

A news crew's interview at a Canadian hospital was cut short yesterday when a man accused of filming up a woman's skirt ran past and was restrained by a pair of good Samaritans.

2 **Man who stabbed ex's fish gets probation**

Reportedly told police: 'If she can't have me, then she can't have the fish'

(Associated Press, October 13, 2009)

A Portland man who attacked his ex-girlfriend and impaled her pet fish this summer has been sentenced to two years probation, a psychological evaluation and community service.

3 **Groom insists he wed absent star**

(www.independent.ie, February 1, 2013)

THE mystery over Gina Lollobrigida's 'fake wedding' deepened last night after her former lover insisted he had legitimately married the Italian film star, despite her not being at the ceremony.

4 **Hiccups soldier killed by comrade**

(www.independent.ie, February 1, 2013)

A US soldier has admitted involuntary manslaughter after shooting his friend accidentally while trying to scare away his hiccups.

Further reading

Conboy, M. 2012. *Journalism Studies: The Basics*, London and New York, Routledge.

Craig, D.A. 2011. *Excellence in Online Journalism: Exploring Current Practices in an Evolving Environment*, Thousand Oaks CA, Sage.

Herbert, J. 2000. *Journalism in the Digital Age,* Oxford, Focal Press.

Lenhart, A., Purcell, K., Smith, A., and Zickuhr, K. 2010. *Social Media and Mobile Internet Use among Teens and Young Adults*, Washington DC, Pew Research Center.

McKane, A. 2006. *Newswriting*, London, Sage.

Pape, S., and Featherstone, S. 2005. *Newspaper Journalism: A Practical Introduction*, London, Sage.

Pavlik, J.V. 2001. *Journalism and New Media*, New York, Columbia University Press.

Reah, D. 2002. *The Language of Newspapers*, London, Routledge.

Rudin, R., and Ibbotson, T. 2002. *An Introduction to Journalism*, Oxford, Focal Press.

Saltzis, K., and Dickinson, R. 2007. 'Inside the changing newsroom: journalists' responses to media convergence', *ASLIB Proceedings*, 60, 3, 216–28.

Sparks, C. 1999. 'The press', in J. Stokes and A. Reading (eds), *The Media in Britain: Current Debates and Developments*, London, Macmillan, 41–60.

Wilkinson, J.S., Grant, A.E., and Fisher, D.J. 2009. *Principles of Convergent Journalism*, New York and Oxford, Oxford University Press.

Chapter 2

Defining news

This chapter provides a definition of news and explains how various factors contribute to making an event newsworthy: for example, the time of the reporting, the location of the event, the availability of pictures and multimedia, etc. The chapter also discusses how the aim of writing objectively, as part of journalists' code of ethics, is shaped by language, audience and technology. Finally, it illustrates the difference between hard news and soft news.

2.1 Defining journalism and news

Journalism can be defined as the reporting of information about recent events through the media.

'News' is the key word in journalism. It encompasses the ideas of *new* and *interesting*, because it refers to the relaying of events that are both recent and relevant. But what can be considered interesting or relevant? Different people have different interests, and those interests vary according to such factors as personal preferences and beliefs, daily experiences, political viewpoints, social and economic conditions, upbringing and education. However, despite the heterogeneity of interests observable among individuals, some people are likely to have a commonality of interests because of their shared background and group membership: i.e., because they are members of the same community. This reflects shared culture, values, experiences and views on facts and events. When journalists create stories for their audiences, they select and prioritize information by reference to what they assume is the common core of beliefs and experiences their audiences share. When an event is considered interesting enough to an audience to be worth including in the paper, the event is said to be *newsworthy*.

2.2 What is newsworthy?

Not all events are considered relevant enough to make it into the paper. So what makes a story potentially newsworthy? A few primary factors determine this.

2.2.1 *Timeliness*

In news reporting, **timeliness** – being ready to report promptly – is one of the determining factors in assigning news value. Timeliness pervades many aspects of news creation and delivery. News is defined by time. A potentially interesting event, reported at the wrong time, is bad news, but an unexciting event can be reported anyway if it occurs at the right time. So stories that could make it to the first page on a quiet day may be buried if they coincide with a hugely important event; this overshadowing of other events often happens with large-scale disasters, such as floods, earthquakes, fires or air crashes. Conversely, stories that might be ignored on a busy news day may be given disproportionate prominence in quiet times. Time also determines the audience's interest in a news story: stories typically attract a lot of attention when they first come out, but then lose their appeal as time goes by.

Finally, timing also rules the life of newspapers themselves. They operate essentially on a 24-hour news cycle. They are printed once a day, typically at night, and once the paper has gone to the press, a story must wait for the next issue to come out, and must compete with all the other news stories. This makes readers anxious to know about the latest events lean towards radio, TV and the Internet, which are designed to break news faster than newspapers. And when newspapers come out with their stories, these media can rely on their audience having information about the story from other sources, and can thus offer a deeper analysis of the events.

2.2.2 *Location*

In any community, certain events are likely to trigger more interest than others. Typically, events occurring within a community, or close by, are more likely to arouse interest than those in distant places: people are more likely to care about what happens in their own backyard than about far-away incidents. So **location** – proximity to the scene of the event – is a determining factor in assigning news value. Proximity does not have to be geographical, though: it can be ideological or political. For example, with regard to the language in which readers have been educated, Australians can relate more to news coming from countries where English is the first language than to news from Asian countries that are closer geographically but where languages other than English are spoken.

Because the news value of an event varies according to how close it is perceived to be, it follows that in different parts of the world, different events get prioritized and assigned news relevance. This is done precisely to comply with the interests of the audience. Comparing the front pages of newspapers published in different geographical areas on any given day will show how location determines news value. Even events that are supposed to have worldwide resonance may be given different priority in different locations around the world. For example, Figure 2.1 shows four newspaper front pages that were published on August 13, 2012, the day after the closing ceremony of the 2012 Olympic Games in London. This was a major event for all the countries that participated, and particularly for the UK, the host country.

Obviously, in the UK the Olympic Games were major news for their whole duration, and they dominated the front pages of local, regional and national papers. The image at the top left of Figure 2.1 is from a UK newspaper, the *Independent*. On this front page, the closing ceremony of the Games is the only news in focus. A picture of the Olympic Stadium, fully illuminated for the occasion, occupies the entire page, with just a few words deemed enough to comment on the event ('That's all folks', the catchphrase on the banner at the end of the Warner Bros' *Looney Tunes* cartoons). A subhead, 'London 2012: Souvenir Edition' makes reference to the special supplement contained in the paper. Under the big picture 'Thanks for the warm-up' repeats the slogan proclaimed by British TV station Channel 4 in a much-applauded advertising campaign for the Paralympic Games, which began the day the Olympics ended. The closing ceremony, often represented by a big picture of the lit-up Olympic Stadium, was in fact the only news most British newspapers considered worth covering on their front pages that day (see www.frontpagestoday.co.uk/2012/08/13/archive.cfm).

The image at the top right of Figure 2.1 is from the *China Daily*, a Chinese newspaper that publishes in English. The Chinese were big players in the Olympic Games and in fact gained medals in many sports. For this reason the paper gives major emphasis to the role of Chinese athletes, showing pictures of several of them and entitling the main piece on the front page 'MOMENTS TO REMEMBER'. Below this is an article discussing the importance for athletes of being able to communicate in English ('Athletes feel English gives them inside track'). In addition to the news about the Olympics, on the same page are two stories that are not related to the Olympics: one discusses work permits; the other state bank funding. Finally, a few stories are given less relevance and placed as a list in the bottom-left corner of the page. Among them is the news of an earthquake in Iran, killing 300 people – which is considered major news in the two other front pages, described below.

The front page at the bottom left of Figure 2.1 is from the *Gulf News*, a paper published in Dubai. This, too, covers the Olympics on the front page.

The INDEPENDENT

That's all, folks

London 2012: Souvenir Edition

THANKS FOR THE WARM-UP

ORDINARY SUSPECT

OLD WORLD APPEAL

Historic sites in Suzhou to get private investment

OLYMPIC SPIRIT

Paralympic athletes set to display talents in London

CHINA DAILY

'New law' focuses on work permits

Draft legislation under review targets negligent employers

MOMENTS TO REMEMBER

IN THE NEWS

Athletes feel English gives them inside track

State bank funding to help major firms go private

Monday

gulfnews.com

GULF NEWS

Golden Olympic moments

How to choose an active investment manager

Women under 18 are now ruling Hollywood

Iran quake toll tops 200

Egypt retires army chief in shake-up

PRESIDENT SCRAPS SWEEPING POWERS FOR THE MILITARY

UAE to send urgent aid to Rohingyas

Asian cities feel the strain

8%

Dh201,140 in traffic fines

Tapping the Ryan agenda

Gen Y and the auto industry

GLOBAL TIMES

DISCOVER CHINA, DISCOVER THE WORLD

Your Great Marketing Opportunity In China...

Nation

Together, apart

6

InDepth

Conjugal rights at building sites

12-13

Life

Express yourself

15

Business

Road rage

20

Scene of devastation

Elusive armed robber confounds police

Nationwide hunt underway for killer

Korea slams Japan plan over disputed islets as imprudent

Inside

Figure 2.1 Comparison of four newspaper front pages from August 13, 2012: the *Independent*[1], UK (top left); the *China Daily*[2], China (top right); the *Gulf News*[3], United Arab Emirates (bottom left); the *Global Times*[4], China (bottom right).

The Games were in fact quite important for the nation: the United Arab Emirates sent 26 athletes to compete, including its football team – more than to any previous competition in which UAE athletes had participated. News about the Olympics occupies a large section of the top part of the page, but the paper gives great prominence also to the Iranian earthquake that struck on August 11, destroying entire villages (as shown in the picture in the middle of the page) and causing many deaths, as well as to the surprise retirement of the Egyptian defence minister (story centre-right of the page). Weight is also given to news of UAE aid sent to the Rohingya Muslims being persecuted in Myanmar (lower portion of the page).

Finally, at the bottom right of Figure 2.1 is the front page from the *Global Times*, another Chinese newspaper published in English. Unlike the *China Daily*, this paper did not consider the Olympic closing ceremony worth major exposure on the front page; its reference to the Games is in one line in the 'Inside' section box in the bottom right-hand corner of the page. Most of the page is occupied by a picture of an Iranian sitting in despair on the ruins of his village, destroyed by the earthquake. Below that, considerable importance is given to the nationwide hunt for a killer (bottom-left portion of the page), and slightly less to news of a dispute over some islands between Korea and Japan. Clearly, for its front page, this paper decided to focus more on events that were geographically closer than the London Olympics.

As the comparison of these four front pages shows, location is a major factor in assigning newsworthiness to events, but this may interact with other factors that could have an impact too. The concept of location has a different meaning when applied to online news. When news goes online, it can be read from any corner of the world, and by an audience that is very heterogeneous in terms of cultural, social or linguistic norms, type of education, etc. So how do online news sources deal with their global audiences? Today most newspapers tend to transpose and adapt the print publication to the web format, assuming the same audience for both print and online editions (see section 2.3.2). In fact, they publish a large amount of the same news in both versions of their papers. However, in future it may be that more online news sources will target an international audience: papers may start to broaden their appeal to distant readers as a way to get more foreign advertising, and so more revenues from the global market. Should that happen, the idea of target audience may have to be reconsidered.

2.2.3 *Topic and familiarity*

What topics are likely to make it to the paper? At a simple level, any **topic** is potentially subject matter for news. However, some lend themselves better than others to being regarded as news, as they may contain an element that is likely to surprise, excite, move the audience, and at the same time provoke discussion and debate. Typically, events that occur less often are considered more newsworthy than more common events. So, for example, a jumbo jet taking off is no news, but a jumbo jet crashing, unarguably, is news. In many cases, judgments of the relevance of a certain event are directly related to the magnitude of its consequences for individuals in society: the greater the consequences, the higher the news value of the event. Thus, the news of two people dying in a fire is going to have less impact on the public than the news of a fire causing the loss of hundreds of lives.

Familiarity – that is, the degree to which the person talked about in the news is known to the audience – is also important. While any pregnant woman makes no news, Angelina Jolie expecting twins makes it to the first page of most US and international magazines. Like most other factors affecting news relevance, familiarity is relative to the targeted audience, as personal and cultural experiences may differ substantially across individuals. Consider, for example, these two headlines:

1 **Shahid Kapoor gains weight and loses film**
(timesofindia.indiatimes.com, October 7, 2012)

2 **Lie Sang-bong, inspired by 'dancheong'**[5]
(www.koreatimes.co.kr, October 7, 2012)

Headline 1 introduces a story about an Indian actor who often appears in Bollywood films. He is well known to people who watch Indian movies and to the Indian audience in general. However, people not familiar with Bollywood movies will be left wondering who he is, and may have little interest in the news story. Similarly, Headline 2 introduces a story about a Korean fashion designer, who was inspired by his traditional Korean pottery to design the collection he presented in London in 2012. The headline may appear rather obscure to readers not into fashion design, or who do not know of this particular designer, or do not know what *dancheong* is.

2.2.4 Pictures and multimedia

The rapid development of information technologies in recent decades and the process of media convergence (see Chapter 1, section 1.7) have had a profound impact on news selection and creation. With the blurring of distinctions between what were originally different media forms, news stories are increasingly selected and 'produced' as media events – i.e. on the basis of their visual, as much as their lexical-verbal appeal. The press, too, has become a highly visual phenomenon. This means that news representations need to create a strong visual impact, by incorporating images relating to the reported event, people and situation. Images can be selected from a number of possible options, including photographs, diagrams, graphic illustrations, satirical cartoons, etc.; on the web, the visual experience is enhanced by audiovisual material. Full-colour images and audiovisual material, often chosen for their dramatic potential, can express immediately what it may take several paragraphs to say in words.

The emphasis on the visual aspects of the story has a direct impact on its perceived newsworthiness: the availability of **pictures** enhances the chances of a story being considered newsworthy. Pictures add vividness and realism and increase the readership's desire to read it. Not all pictures will do, though: pictures about famous and/or attractive people are more likely to lead to the writing up of news. So, for example, news may be created around pictures of celebrities caught wearing extravagant outfits, or engaged in some unusual activity. Pictures may also contribute to the dramatization of a story and to the creation of its 'protagonist', particularly when the photograph is appealing. As in many media events, the young, the cute, the gorgeous and the extraordinary have greater chances of being considered newsworthy than the ugly or the ordinary. 'Sadly, a missing teenager has more chance of making the front page if there's a good quality-picture of her looking sweet and pretty' (Wolstenholme, reported by Pape and Featherstone, 2005: 20). This happened, for example, in the case of Rebecca Caine discussed in Chapter 5. Her fatal accident is recounted in detail in a rather long story, but what draws the attention of readers is the big close-up picture of the young, blond and gorgeous model accompanying the story.

2.2.5 Dramatic potential

News stories aim to create an impact on the reader. This is often an aspect of the type of story that is told. Some stories lend themselves better than others to being communicated vividly and make a lasting impression on the audience. Such stories contain elements known to make a compelling narrative that connects deeply and on a profoundly personal level with media audiences: for example, innocent victims, brutal killers, personal tragedies, etc. Stories containing some of these elements are said to have **dramatic potential.**

The dramatic potential of a story contributes to its newsworthiness. That is because tragic and dramatic events, like deaths, are considered more newsworthy than happy events like marriages – unless the marriage concerns some celebrity. Brutal actions like rape and murder trigger an immediate feeling of sympathy in the reader; also, because of their emotional impact, they are rather easy to understand and absorb, and do not require detailed explanations or interpretations. In this sense, dramatic events are unlike economic, social or cultural trends, which tend to evolve over long periods of time, are more complex to explain and understand, and lack the potential for sensationalism that tragic events have. The story about Milly Dowler and the serial killer discussed in Chapter 9 provides a good example of a violent story in which the dramatic potential has been exploited to arouse readers' interest.

Often, when the news is not highly dramatic *per se*, the language of the report will boost its dramatic potential, so as to enhance its chances of attracting readers' attention. The headlines below give some examples of dramatic language used for news that is not intrinsically dramatic.

1 **High school football: A dramatic turnaround at Cupertino**
(www.mercurynews.com, October 3, 2012)

2 **Cancer death rates set for a 'dramatic fall'**
(www.bbc.co.uk, September 25, 2012)

3 **The war on boys: Young men losing ground in education, emotional health and jobs**
(www.deseretnews.com, February 19, 2012)

4 **Machynlleth: The town whose heart is broken**
(www.independent.co.uk, October 7, 2012)

5 **Greek tragedy**
(www.nytimes.com, May 12, 2012)

In all the examples, the language chosen gives an aura of sensationalism to otherwise plain headlines: in examples 1 and 2 this is done through the use of the adjective *dramatic*; example 3 uses a metaphor (*The war on boys*) to introduce a story about problems with boys' education, emotional health and employment; likewise, example 4 uses a metaphor (*The town whose heart is broken*) to introduce a story about a missing girl; and, finally, in example 5 a learned word association (*Greek tragedy)* is used to talk about the economic situation affecting Greece.

2.2.6 *General interest, seasonal and trendy topics*

Finally, events are considered newsworthy when they are of **general interest** to the target readership (e.g., national elections, the death of a prime minister), affect a lot of people (e.g., a jumbo jet crash, a storm, an earthquake), are **seasonal** (e.g., traffic before big holidays, end-of-the-school-year exams, new trends during the summer season), or are truly extraordinary (e.g., the discovery of an ancient treasure, the fattest man on earth). News that is received with a lot of interest from the public tends to generate interest in similar following news. In this sense, news and media events tend to feed on themselves. This is often true of gossip about celebrities, as well as sad and disturbing events such as children's abductions, which are likely to magnetize readers' attention and may be used by newspapers as a device to increase the paper's sales and circulation.

Here are some examples of news considered to be of general interest:

1 **Mainlanders face new traffic crush as travellers return from long holiday**
(www.scmp.com, October 6, 2012)

2 **More floods, slides loom. Tropical depression spotted off N. Luzon**
(*Philippine Daily Inquirer*, August 13, 2012)

3 **In Russia, boy finds intact carcass of 30,000-yr-old woolly mammoth**
(timesofindia.indiatimes.com, October 6, 2012)

4 **Halloween frenzy takes over**
(www.hindustantimes.com, October 27, 2005)

2.3 Objectivity in news reporting: a factor of language, audience and technology

Unlike fiction writers or storytellers, journalists are committed to a **code of ethics**, defined by the principles of truthfulness, accuracy, objectivity, impartiality and fairness in news reporting. But what *is* objectivity in this context, and can journalists be truly fair and balanced?

Objectivity in news reporting means that journalists report information that is true and factual, avoid political ideology and partisanship, and refrain from conveying personal feelings and prejudices or expressing personal opinions. As part of this process, journalists research the information they report and cite their sources, so as to add credibility to their stories (see Chapter 3).[6]

However, it is safe to assume that journalists cannot be truly objective. Besides personal ideology, at least three factors shape how news is reported by a journalist: language, audience and technology.

2.3.1 Language

Reporters strive to use neutral **language** to tell their stories. But language is itself a social construct and cannot be neutral. As we shall see later (Chapters 6–9), journalists make lexical and grammatical choices, both consciously and unconsciously, that reflect their ideology. And ideology also conditions readers' interpretation of news texts. In other words, news texts are subjectively written and subjectively interpreted.

A typical example is the use of adjectives, which can betray the writers' judgment on the narrated event. Thus, in a hypothetical article describing a clash between a group of protesters and the police, the use of expressions like those in 1 below to refer to the protesters is an indication that the journalist is critical of the group's actions.

1 The *ruthless* nature of the militants
The *horrifying* tactic
The *brutality* of the protesters

Similarly, in a sentence like that in 2 the contrast between the *assault* action of the rioters and the *innocent* bystander presents a view in which all the blame is laid on the rioters. On the other hand, in 3 the emphasis is on the eruption of rage following an action by Guatemalan police (the killing of 6 protesters) said to be part of an *excessive* use of force against the protesters and condemned by the human-rights groups.

2 **Rioters assault innocent bystander with fire extinguisher**
(www.foxnews.com, August 18, 2011)

3 **Rage erupts in Guatemala after police kill 6 protesters**
Human rights groups condemned the government's actions and charged they were part of a pattern of excessive use of force against protesters.
(adapted from: www.mansfieldnewsjournal.com, October 5, 2012)

2.3.2 *Audience*

Audience is the second major factor affecting news presentation and delivery. As we saw in Chapter 1, news agencies are economic institutions, and their goal is to generate revenues. Advertisers and media corporations exert pressure on journalists to boost profits by appealing to large audiences. Because of this, newspapers cater to their audiences: editorial decisions, topic selection and presentation of events, the amount of detail in the story, the pictures and images accompanying it, all reflect the perceived needs of a target audience.

Thus, journalists must write with their audience in mind, and they do so on the basis of a set of common values that they assume to be shared with the audience. The level of sophistication of the language also varies according to the target audience, with journalists adapting their styles and vocabulary choices to suit the expected readership.

In many countries the daily newspaper market is divided into broadsheets and tabloids. **Broadsheets** typically cover the most important national and international news, and are written using formal language with a sober tone. **Tabloids** provide less in-depth news and give more coverage to gossip, entertainment and sports news; they are written in casual, informal language, with extensive use of slang and an often-irreverent tone. By selecting their topics and using different language styles, broadsheets and tabloids reflect their aims to appeal to two different kinds of (stereotyped) readerships: an educated middle-class audience for the former, a less-educated working-class audience for the latter (see also Chapter 4).

An example of the front pages of two US tabloids is given in Figure 2.2. Both are characterized by big pictures, huge characters and the use of informal and colloquial language. This is intended to have a strong visual as well as textual impact on the reader. The two tabloids cover local news or gossip rather than nationally or internationally relevant news. By contrast, broadsheets make a less strong visual impact on the audience by using smaller images, smaller headlines, more text and more formal language, because they are seeking to appeal to a readership with higher education than the tabloid audience. (For examples of broadsheet front pages see Figure 2.1 on page 28.)

In general, the online editions of most newspapers are targeted at the same type of audience as the print edition, and preserve some of the characteristics of the print papers. Accordingly, the web pages of some well-known tabloids (e.g., www.mirror.co.uk/; www.thesun.co.uk/; www.mid-day.com/; www.dailystar.co.uk/home/; www.nationalenquirer.com/; weeklyworldnews.com/; www.dailymail.co.uk/; www.dailymail.co.uk/indiahome/index.html) differ from the web pages of well-known broadsheets (e.g., www.thetimes.co.uk/; www.guardiannews.com/; www.nytimes.com/; www.wsj.com/; timesofindia.indiatimes.com/; www.atimes.com/). While the former tend to have large characters and images and sensationalistic headlines, the latter have a sober tone, with smaller characters, smaller pictures and more factual headlines.

SPECIAL REPORT: FEAR ON OUR STREETS

BOSTON Herald

'WHAT THE HECK IS GOING ON OUT THERE?'

HESLAM: PALS MOURN DEATH OF 'SWEETHEART' MANHUNT FOR RUTHLESS KILLERS

SPORTS FINAL

DAILY NEWS

NEW YORK'S HOMETOWN NEWSPAPER

Taylor splashes $5M for love

EXCLUSIVE PHOTO

SEE PAGES 8–9

GONE IN 60 SECONDS!

Duped driver's $150G car is swiped in Times Sq. – while he looks on!

Figure 2.2 The front pages of two US tabloids: the *Boston Herald*[7] (left) and the *Daily News*[8] (right).

2.3.3 Technology and multimodal communication

As we have seen in section 2.2.4, the availability of low-cost multimedia and the desire to make a strong impact on the audience determine not only *how* stories are covered, but also *what* stories are covered. In other words, news stories may be selected on the basis of what videos or images are available, rather than on their intrinsic news value in the absence of such material.

The fact that the visual element is so pervasive in the media raises the question of how we access the meaning of the different elements (i.e., images, audiovisual and language) in the text.

Research has shown that communication occurs across more than a single mode of expression, which makes it inherently **multimodal**. This means that in face-to-face conversation, for example, the meaning is exchanged not only through words, but also through other semiotic resources, such as gestures, facial expressions, intonation, gaze, etc. It is in fact the interaction and integration of all the different modes of discourse that creates meaning and shapes the interpretation of communication. This is exemplified in the expression: *It is not* what *you say, but* how *you say it!*

In media texts, visual and non-verbal elements (photographs, videos, diagrams and graphics) integrate with verbal elements (spoken or written words) in the expression of meaning. Images and visual information enhance and facilitate the flow of information and the reception of the message. However, the meanings created by the visual elements in a text are often more implicit or indirect than language. Thus, in general, the textual message directs the interpretation of the visual message, and the text creator may use language to point the reader towards a particular interpretation of the visual. As with any other intervention of news selection and presentation, photographic material can be cropped or digitally manipulated to magnify details, cut out context, etc., and thus provide a key to a particular interpretation of the text.

When a text has no images, it will still be perceived as a form of communication with its own characteristics, and one that differs from spoken language. This is due to the particular features of design (page layout, type and size of fonts, use of colours) that are associated with it, and that may be conventionally recognized by the reader as characterizing specific genres. For example, news articles come in a distinct format, which is immediately recognized by the reader as being part of the genre 'news'. This will be discussed in Chapter 4.

2.4 Hard news and soft news

A distinction is made between two categories of news stories: hard news and soft news.

Hard news includes stories concerning events that have just happened or are about to happen. Though hard news often deals with catastrophic or life-threatening events, such as crimes, wars and disasters, it can also simply deal with politics or economics: for example, the results of recent elections, significant public statements, new tax laws, etc. It is hard news that fills most of newspapers' front pages. Typically, a hard-news story provides an account of the facts, as well as the reasons and implications for the readership (the *who*, *what*, *why*, *when*, *where* and *how* of an event). The characteristic style of hard news is the 'Inverted Pyramid' (see Chapter 5), where the event outcome is told at the beginning of the story, while background, detailed information about its circumstances is provided in decreasing order of importance. A type of hard news is the so-called **breaking news**, which refers to unexpected events – such as plane crashes or major earthquakes – developing or occurring shortly before the publication deadline that reporters feel they need to cover as quickly as possible, interrupting scheduled programming and/or current news to do so.

Soft news has a focus on 'human interest' and generally concerns less immediate, life-changing events, such as arts and entertainment, sports, lifestyle and celebrities. It may originate simply from a reporter's curiosity about a topic: for example, an article about new gadgets to buy, 'The hottest sets of wheels and hi-tech gizmos', which appeared on September 4, 2005, in indiatoday.intoday.in, is unmistakably soft news.

Soft news that focuses on people or issues that affect readers' lives is called 'feature stories'. For example, an item about the consequences of increasing air pollution levels could be considered a feature story. It is no less important than hard news, but, unlike hard news, it has not happened overnight. Most feature stories arise from a news event, but, rather than providing just a factual account of the event, they offer the opportunity for further investigations or opinions, often focusing on human reactions and presenting quotations from people.

Audiences want hard news to be informed about what is happening around the world and in their community. But they also want soft news to feed their general knowledge, to entertain them and to satisfy their curiosity.

Students' activities

Activity 1

Access the Newseum site (www.newseum.org/todaysfrontpages/), a virtual Museum collecting over 800 newspapers' front pages from 91 countries daily, shown in alphabetical order).

Compare the front pages of a few newspapers on the same day. Explain how the differences between them may reflect differences in the target audiences' culture, geographical position, political viewpoint, etc.

Activity 2

Compare a print newspaper with its online version. Pick one story that has been covered by both media. Compare the overall content; do a word count; look at how links are used in the online version and how multimedia is used to enhance the story. Explain how the two versions differ.

Activity 3

We have seen in this chapter that the type of audience different newspapers target has an effect on the language and content of the news. The following excerpts, taken from two British papers on February 1, 2013, deal with the news of British football-player David Beckham signing a contract to play for free in Paris. Compare the two excerpts and analyse how the language used reflects differences in the papers' target readerships. In particular, look at differences in: the use of informal vs. formal words and expressions; the use of colloquialisms; the use of foreign words; the use of sentence structure (does one of the texts use sentences that are more complex than the other's?).

1 Becks, 37, dubbed Le Spice Boy by adoring fans in the French capital, will give every penny of his £150,000-a-week salary to needy children.
   GENEROUS David Beckham signed a multi-million pound deal to join French side Paris St Germain yesterday – and promised every penny to needy kids.

(*Daily Star*, February 1, 2013)

2 [...] the player French journalists know as "Le Spice Boy" stepped on to the Paris stage. With his blond highlights slicked back, tattoos poking out of his sharp suit, David Beckham flashed his trademark polite, white smile and uttered the one word of French he said he knew: "Bonjour".

(the *Guardian*, February 1, 2013)

Activity 4

The two headlines below come from reports of the story, discussed above, about David Beckham signing a contract to play in Paris. Both are from *The Times* of London: the first appeared in the print edition, the second in the online edition. Compare the two and reflect on the possible reasons why such different headlines were chosen for the two editions.

1 **Alors, sur ma tête, mon fils**

(*The Times*, February 1, 2013)

2 **David Beckham delighted with Paris match**

(www.thetimes.co.uk, February 1, 2013)

Further reading

Durant, A., and Lambrou, M. 2009. *Language and Media: A Resource Book for Students*, London and New York, Routledge.
Herbert, J. 2000. *Journalism in the Digital Age*, Oxford, Focal Press.
Lacey, C., and Longman, D. 1997. *The Press as Public Educator: Cultures of Understanding, Cultures of Ignorance*, Luton, University of Luton.
Rudin, R., and Ibbotson, T. 2002. *An Introduction to Journalism*, Oxford, Focal Press.
Stuart Adams, G. 2002. 'Notes toward a definition of journalism', in R.P. Clark and C.C. Campbell (eds), *The Values and Craft of American Journalism*, Gainesville, University Press of Florida, 7–40.

Chapter 3

Sourcing news

This chapter explains how news reporters gather the information for their stories from a variety of different sources, and then write their articles by combining the resulting pieces of information, quoting some sources and paraphrasing others. It also reviews what sources are commonly used to create news stories and how the information gathered from the sources is integrated into the text.

3.1 News stories need sources

Preparing a news story involves a first phase of investigation, observation of events and/or interviews with people. Stories are then created by putting together all the information collected into a coherent piece. The practice of locating and using a person or publication to provide information that will be used for news stories is called 'sourcing'. **Sourcing** is a basic tool in news reporting, as it allows journalists to pursue objectivity and fairness, two basic principles in the journalistic code of ethics.

3.2 Sourcing the news

Reporters use various types of **sources** to gather the information they need for their stories, and are expected to develop and cultivate sources as part of their profession. Moreover, they are often short of time, so it is essential to cut the time needed to get to reliable and available sources, and one of the reporter's basic tools is a contact database, which contains a list of source names and any detail that would be helpful to remember.

Conventional journalistic practices divide sources between on-diary and off-diary sources. Broadly speaking, **on-diary sources** are those reporters contact as part of their routine activities, among them people or bodies that may provide breaking news or news updates. On-diary sources include, at the local level, the police, the fire brigade, schools and community groups, city council members, business leaders; at the national level they will include bodies of the government and the parliament, major political parties, trade unions. **Off-diary sources**, those that journalists do not contact as part of their daily routine, are used when unanticipated events arise. They may include other media and news agencies; specialist journals; newspaper cuttings; and witnesses, who may provide details through personal accounts.

Journalists also draw information from a wide variety of written sources, including: local, public and university libraries; their own newspaper archives of clippings of items previously published in the paper; trusted internet sites (e.g., national institutes of health, government sites); commercial databases compiled by private companies; public records (e.g., real-estate records, tax payment records, police records, school district records); mailing lists and newsgroups.

In recent years, news organizations have shown a tendency to reduce the economic resources (e.g., staffing, specialist correspondents, foreign bureau) necessary to do investigative journalism and create lengthy and in-depth stories. This is due to the pressure to make profits and the competition from the number of accessible news sources, and it affects both traditional and online journalism. Faced with these challenges, journalists are increasingly taking advantage of new technology to ground their reporting by searching for documents online, and making use of all digital resources.

3.3 Interviews

Interviews are one of the traditional methods used for gathering information for a news story. Talking to the people who are directly involved in the story event is considered the best way to find out the truth about the event itself. According to Rich (2003: 92): 'News writing needs human sources to make the story credible and readable. Information from eyewitnesses and participants lends immediacy to the story, and direct quotes make a story interesting.'

Reporters typically prepare for interviews by conducting research on the source's background and the story subject. This helps them ask the source the right set of questions. Different types of story may need different types of interview. For example, a face-to-face interview is preferable in the case of sensitive subjects, or when a detailed description of the source is to be included in the story. In fact, face-to-face interviews allow the interviewer to establish a rapport with the interviewee, and to gather information, through personal observation, about their surroundings. Alternatively, interviews that can be done from the work desk, by phone or email, save the reporter a lot of time but are more impersonal. Using emails the reporter also loses control of the timing, because of the risk of having to wait for answers for an undetermined amount of time.

3.4 Reporting news sources

3.4.1 *Attribution*

Journalistic practices require journalists to attribute information to its source: that is, to tell readers where the information comes from. Attributions are found throughout news stories and are used to report any information that is not common knowledge. Only when the information presented in the story can be considered indisputable or shared by the general public, can attribution be omitted. Attributions are important because they add authenticity and authority to a story, and they empower readers to judge the quality of the information reported and whether it comes from an impartial or a biased observer.

Generally, attributions provide a complete identification of the source when it is first mentioned. For example, human sources are usually introduced by their full name and job title (when relevant) in the first reference, though subsequent references may use only the last name. In other cases, when full attribution is deemed cumbersome and liable to clutter the text, sources may be introduced by a generic title (e.g., 'Police/Police Chief'), with fuller identification delayed to a later paragraph (e.g., 'Chief Johnson').

Source qualifications are added preferentially to people whose knowledge in the field is recognized by a public or private institution (e.g., the local town chief police officer, the school principal, the company's director), or to people considered experts in the field (such as university professors, scientists, etc.). This is done to provide opinions that can be agreed upon because they are considered highly valuable, authoritative and independent. When their views are being presented, the sources act as spokespersons for the group or institution they represent. This helps reporters strengthen the credibility and value of the story. On the other hand, sources that are unnamed or have no title or representative function are considered weak sources, because their views and opinions cannot be identified with those of a larger group. However, reporters will use sources with no qualifications when necessary: i.e., when no other sources are available. One kind of unqualified source often used in news reporting is eyewitnesses, who may provide valuable details about events for which no information is available on the record.

The story below, about the demolition of the house of China's last emperor, published in the online version of *China Daily* in August 2012, provides a nice range of examples of how sources can be used in a news story.

China's last emperor's house demolished[1]

(chinadaily.com.cn, August 15, 2012)

1 The residence of Aisin-Gioro Puyi (1906-67), the last ruler of China, has become a pile of rubble, Beijing News reported.
2 The Western-style house, built during the Republic of China (1912–49) period in Beijing, was torn down for potential safety problems due to rainstorm damage, according to Sun Tiexiang, an official from the house and land management center of Xicheng district.
3 'The house does not belong to historic buildings and has not been listed as a heritage conservation unit,' Sun said. But it will be rebuilt on the same site, he said.
4 Chen Guangzhong, a writer of culture and history, showed his regret about the destruction of the old house. 'The place is a witness to an emperor turning into a citizen of the People's Republic of China,' he said.
5 Puyi, the last emperor of the Qing Dynasty (1644–1911), lived in the house with his wife, Li Shuxian, from 1963 until his death in 1967. His abdication in 1912 marked the end of centuries of imperial rule in China.

In this story, the source of the news of the last emperor's house demolition is attributed to *Beijing News* (paragraph 1). The reason why the house was torn down is reported as given by an expert authority, *Sun Tiexiang, an official from the house and land management center of Xicheng district*. The expert is introduced with full name and qualifications in paragraph 2, but simply referred to by his last name, *Sun*, or a pronoun, *he*, in paragraph 3.

In paragraph 4, the opinion that it may have been a cultural mistake to destroy the emperor's house is expressed through the words of another expert, *Chen Guangzhong, a writer of culture and history*. Finally, in paragraph 5, information about the life and death of the last emperor of the Qing Dynasty is given that includes Puyi's dates of birth and death, date of abdication, and when he lived in the house; this information is given no attribution, being considered easily available, indisputable and general knowledge.

In attributions, job titles may be omitted when a source is well known to the general public – as, for instance, celebrities, important politicians, well-known Nobel Prize winners, etc. (e.g., Michael Jackson, Bill Gates, Barack Obama, Wen Jiabao, Einstein, Aung San Suu Kyi). When the audience might not be familiar with the sources, attribution is usually given. This is illustrated in the two examples below: in 1 full attribution is given to the Russian Prime Minister because his recent election might not have been enough to make him well known to the audience outside of Russia; in 2 neither Elton John nor Madonna needs an attribution, as the two celebrities are assumed to be well known to the general public.

1 **Russian Prime Minister Dmitry Medvedev has called for three members of the punk band Pussy Riot to be freed, saying further prison time would be 'unproductive'.**

(Associated Press, September 12, 2012)

2 **Elton John has reignited his public spat with Madonna, calling her a 'fairground stripper' whose career is over.**

(www.timesofmalta.com, August 8, 2012)

3.4.2 Anonymous sources

In some cases, stories may present anonymous or unqualified sources (e.g., *sources near the president said … , Royal insiders say …*). This may be due to the reporter's commitment to keeping the source's name concealed. In fact, for a source to be assured that his/her name will not be reported in the story may be a reason to speak more openly. In general, however, not to mention the source's name and qualification has the effect of decreasing the credibility of the story. For this reason, whenever possible, reporters avoid the use of unnamed sources – those identified with vague references (e.g., *public records suggest … , it has been said …*).

Occasionally sources may be left vague and unspecified on purpose when the information reported in the story has not been verified. This may happen, for example, when the reporter has not been able to check the validity of the sources, due to time constraints. One such case is shown in the excerpt below, concerning the possible death of the Iraqi dictator Saddam Hussein in an air strike, during the frantic timeline of events of the Iraqi war led by the British and US forces (2003–2011). In fact the news turned out to be false; Saddam was actually captured months later and executed years later. The article was written on April 8, 2003, and appeared briefly on the morning edition of MSNBC news (www.msnbc.msn.com). The item was actually posted for less than an hour before being replaced by a piece containing details of the air strike and the people killed in it, which did not mention Saddam.

Airstrike may have killed Saddam[2]

(msnbc.msn.com, April 8, 2003)

1 A US Air Force warplane dropped four enormous bombs Monday on a residential complex where 'extremely reliable' intelligence indicated that Iraqi President Saddam Hussein and one or both of his sons were attending a meeting, senior administration officials told NBC News. The sources would not rule out the possibility that Saddam could have moved before the bomber struck, but they said it was likely that he and his sons were dead.

2 Based on information from an intelligence source on the ground in Baghdad, US military officials were confident that Saddam and his son Qusay were attending a meeting in the neighbourhood with other top Iraqi leaders, senior officials told NBC's Carl Rochelle at the Pentagon and Andrea Mitchell at the State Department. They said they believed it was possible that Saddam's other son, Uday, also was there.

3 The intelligence information was considered so reliable that it justified a massive attack in a residential area of the al-Mansur district of western Baghdad despite the administration's declared emphasis on avoiding civilian casualties, diplomatic and military sources said.

In this story, two features contribute to presenting the news as uncertain: the systematic use of modal expressions to refer to the reported events and the vagueness of the sources, which are left anonymous and unspecified.

The story headline presents the news as tentative through the use of the modal verb *may*. In paragraph 1 (the lead) the news about the bombing comes from anonymous *senior administration officials*, later referred to as *The sources*. The information about the presence of *Saddam Hussein and one or both of his sons* in the residential complex comes from *'extremely reliable' intelligence* (though the quotes may suggest the reporter is not sure of their actual reliability). The final sentence in the lead is especially tentative, as all verb phrases suggest a high level of uncertainty: *The sources would not rule out the possibility that Saddam could have moved before the bomber struck, but they said it was likely that he and his sons were dead.*

The paragraphs following the lead are also characterized by the frequent use of modality and unspecified sources. In paragraph 2, the information is said to come from an anonymous *intelligence source on the ground in Baghdad*, and from *senior officials*. The verbal expressions convey tentativeness: *officials were confident that* ... , *They said they believed it was possible that* ... In paragraph 3 the informants are again anonymous *diplomatic and military sources*; the information is presented as uncertain: *The intelligence information was considered so reliable that* ... In the excerpt, only two people are mentioned, i.e., *NBC's Carl Rochelle at the Pentagon* and *Andrea Mitchell at the State Department*, the two people who collected the information from the sources.

It is indeed possible that some of the sources' names may have been left unspecified because of their role within the US military. However, the references to anonymous sources, together with the many modal verbs, suggest that, when writing the story, the reporter had not verified its truthfulness or did not consider it an accurate report of the events.

As the example shows, attributions are a powerful device to provide indirect information about the story. The next section will discuss how the sources' words can be integrated in the text.

3.4.3 *Quoting sources to create stories*

Sources' information can be quoted directly or indirectly. When they are quoted directly, the sources' words are reported in quotes (''); when quoted indirectly, the sources' words are reported with no quotes, as a subordinate clause to the main clause.[3] The following two sentences illustrate, respectively, the two structures:

> 'I do not believe this is true,' said Dr Thompson. (Direct Quote).
> Dr Thompson said she did not believe that to be true. (Indirect Quote).

Sources' words can also be paraphrased or summarized, as in:

> Dr Thompson was skeptical. (Paraphrase).

In most stories, the information coming from a variety of sources, in the form of direct or indirect quotes or paraphrases, is integrated in the text to create a unified piece.

The story below reports of a man arrested in Georgia (US) for trying to put his wife into the kitchen oven. The article distinguishes between information coming from an authoritative source (Sgt. Jodi Shupe from the Sheriff's Office in Rockdale County, Georgia) and information that has not been proved to be true (what the arrested man, named Jackson, has told the police). The former includes the story of Jackson's arrest and charges, his married life history, his wife's head injuries – possibly verified by Stg. Shupe at the time of Jackson's arrest. The latter comprises reference to all events leading to the man's arrest, i.e., Jackson's fight with his wife and his trying to force her into the oven, which have not yet been verified (*after* allegedly *trying; Jackson* apparently *started fighting; Jackson* allegedly *attempted to stuff his wife*). In these circumstances, the reporter is careful to use the words *allegedly* or *apparently* to suspend any judgment on Jackson, who has not yet officially been proved guilty.

Man Allegedly Tries to Put Wife in Oven[4]

(Associated Press, November 30, 2006)

1 CONYERS, Ga. A man has been arrested after allegedly trying to force his estranged wife into an oven on Thanksgiving in front of their five children.

2 Martin Luther Jackson, 31, of Decatur, has been charged with aggravated assault, aggravated battery, cruelty to children and possession of marijuana after the Nov. 23 incident, said Sgt. Jodi Shupe of the Rockdale County Sheriff's Office.

3 Jackson and his 29-year-old wife, who have been separated since July, have five children ranging in age from 1 to 13 years old, Shupe said. Jackson apparently started fighting with his wife after she and the children returned to their Conyers home on Thanksgiving.
4 At one point during the fight, Jackson allegedly attempted to stuff his wife inside the kitchen oven, which had been left on to heat the house, Shupe said. The woman escaped and went to the sheriff's office with visible head injuries, Shupe said.
5 Investigators found Jackson hiding under a bed at his mother's house in Decatur, where he had been living since the separation, Shupe said.

All the events are reported as indirect quotes. In the first paragraph after the lead, both Jackson and Shupe are introduced with their full names (and titles in the case of Shupe), but they are called only Jackson and Shupe in all later references. Following a common strategy used in news reporting, the quote precedes the attribution, because what is said is more important than who said it. The attribution of the information to the police officer (*Shupe said*) is found in all the paragraphs after the lead, i.e., paragraphs 2–5. The repetition of the same attribution in each paragraph may seem tedious, but it imbues the information given in the story with credibility, which is possibly why it is maintained. The verb *said* – which is the only reporting verb used in this article to report the news – is considered a neutral verb of attribution and is highly favoured in news reporting.

As this chapter has shown, through attribution and speech reporting language offers journalists the means to combine pieces of information, integrate them in their stories and convey their perspective on the truthfulness of what they are reporting. The next chapter will discuss how meaning can be conveyed through the design of the newspaper page.

Students' activities

Activity 1

Access the site of a news network (for example, www.cnn.com/; abcnews.go.com/; www.bbc.co.uk/) and watch a video reporting on a current event. Then look at the same news as it was covered in a print newspaper. Are there differences in the way the broadcast and the print news stories attribute the sources of information? (Look at names, titles and any other detail.)

Activity 2

Compare two or more stories, written in two different countries, on some political or economic event that has international relevance (e.g., the election of the US president; the economic crisis in the EU; the alliance between the leaders of two countries; the leadership transition of the Chinese Communist Party). Observe how the two texts qualify the authorities in the stories. Are the authorities introduced with their full names and titles? (For example, do they simply say: *Cristina Elisabet Fernández de Kirchner*, or do they say: *Argentinian president Cristina Fernández de Kirchner?*). How do the attributions in the articles differ, based on the journalists' assumed knowledge of their audience? What other details in the stories depend on these assumptions?

Activity 3

Compare any two stories on the same topic. Analyse how they differ in the sources they report and the attributions they give.

Activity 4

Imagine a news story that contains the following line:

> The President **suggested** he feels consumers' pain.

The key word here is *suggested*. Other ways in which the writer could have expressed the same idea are:

> The President **said** he feels consumers' pain
> The President **argued** he feels consumers' pain
> The President **expressed that** he feels consumers' pain
> The President **stated that** he feels consumers' pain.
> The President **explained that** he feels consumers' pain.
> The President **responded that** he feels consumers' pain.

However, all of these verbs really express different meanings. What are the meanings expressed by all these verbs? Which can be considered more neutral? Which do you think are used more often in the news?

Activity 5

In Chapter 5, the text on pages 76–8 discusses the nutritional value of pet food. The article is clearly based on a scientific report, but its aim is to be readable by the non-expert reader. Study the article and reconstruct all the different sources of information and analyse how they are attributed.

Further reading

Clark, C. 2012. 'How do we know? *Evidentiality* in British quality newspapers', in F. Dalziel, S. Gesuato and M.T. Musacchio (eds), *A Lifetime of English Studies: Essays in Honour of Carol Taylor Torsello*, Padova, Il Poligrafo, 149–58.

Keeble, R. 2006. *The Newspapers Handbook,* 4th ed., London and New York, Routledge.

National Union of Journalists. *NUJ Code of Conduct*, www.nuj.org.uk/files/NUJ_Code_of_Conduct.pdf.

Pape, S., and Featherstone, S. 2005. *Newspaper Journalism: A Practical Introduction*, London, Sage.

Reuters, *Reuters Handbook of Journalism*, handbook.reuters.com/extensions/docs/pdf/handbookofjournalism.pdf.

Society of Professional Journalists. 1996. *SPJ Code of Ethics*, www.spj.org/ethicscode.asp.

Chapter 4

Conveying meaning through design

The topic here is the design of the newspaper page and how page design represents a powerful form of non-verbal communication, essential for the success of the publication. We then examine what elements contribute to page design (layout, grids, images, texts), and how different types of page design appeal to different audiences.

4.1 Design as the key to a successful publication

Design is as important to a successful publication as well-written text. Through their design, publications attract their audiences and communicate with them. The design guides readers through the publication and enables them to prioritize content and search for information. Intelligent design involves finding a proper balance between content and visual elements, such as shapes, colours and contrasts. Publications that are too dense in text and present little contrast are hard to read, while pages that have too much graphic matter and too little text risk disappointing the reader who is looking for information. Both print and online news strive to find the design that best addresses readers' needs and preferences and, at the same time, best satisfies the strategic objectives of authors and organizations.

This chapter reviews some of the features of page design for both print and online news publications and emphasizes what is common to both.

4.2 Integrating content, editing and design

Design affects every aspect of a publication and is dealt with by every person in the newsroom. As writers develop stories, they keep in mind the best ways to draw the reader into the text by prioritizing some information and, for example, by using appropriate text paragraphing. Editors check the text for accuracy and clarity, assign pictures and graphics to the text, and decide on headlines, story placements and space on the page. Editor designers come in towards the end of the process to integrate texts, graphics and pictures, as well as deciding on a powerful layout (that is, the organization of the elements in the page) using predetermined grids (see section 4.5). Every part of the design – colours, graphics, typography, layout – is chosen for the meanings it conveys. Half the battle is to get the reader to stop on the page. If readers stop on a page, they are more likely to at least browse it and perhaps read something.

Awareness of the importance of design at all stages of news reporting underlies *WED* (Writing, Editing, and Design), a practice that encourages teams of writers, editors, photographers, artists and designers to tell stories in the most effective and vivid way possible. It focuses on how every component of a story, including its design (e.g. photographs and images, colours, typographical choices, and graphics), contributes to the meaning and interpretation of that story, and is chosen precisely so as to convey a specific kind of meaning. For each news story, visual decisions are inspired by the topic at hand, and then applied on the basis of the interpretative slant to be assigned to it.

4.3 Designing a publication for an audience

As happens with any other publication, the editors of a newspaper choose designs to successfully deliver appropriate content to the market segment they address – that is, to comply with the audience's demands. This explains the differences between different types of newspapers: what works for a local or popular paper (e.g., a tabloid) would not necessarily work for authoritative papers targeting educated readerships, like the *Financial Times* or the *New York Times*.

Nowadays, readers have limited time to read. Also, accustomed as they are to fast-flowing images on videos and TV, they have short attention spans. Hence it is important for a publication to plan its design carefully, so as to enhance the processability of news delivery by the impatient readers and, more generally, to maximize its impact on the readership. Decisions regarding publication design are based on studies of the target audience, returning data on the expected readers' age, gender, education and literacy level, income range, geographical area of residence, habits, interests and beliefs, and political viewpoint. This allows the editorial team to design a publication tailored to the audience's preferences, and to use design features, such as colour, layout, typography and images, in such a way as to best represent the lifestyle values associated with that audience.

Advances in digital and print technology (desktop computers, word-processing software, graphics software, digital cameras, digital pre-press and typesetting technologies) have eased publication design and revolutionized the newspaper production process. Compared to fifty years ago, today's print newspaper layouts are more creative, colourful and visually attractive in spite of the unchanged limitations of the print medium, which impose constraints such as the fixed size of the page.

For print papers, different types of design are used with different newspaper formats. A distinction is drawn between **broadsheets**, the largest newspaper format, characterized by long vertical pages (575–600 mm by 380 mm), the **compact** (or **tabloid**) format (380 mm by 300 mm), and the **Berliner** (470 mm by 315 mm). Because of their large size, broadsheets have long been considered the most appropriate format for in-depth stories. Today they still typically target educated readerships, cover all national and international news, provide an in-depth account of events and use formal language. Tabloids have traditionally tended to cover sensationalist and celebrity material, entertainment and sports, using colloquial language and slang – although some respected newspapers, such as *The Times* and the *Independent* among UK newspapers – are in tabloid format. Berliners, a more recent introduction, fall between the broadsheet and the compact/tabloid in their characteristics: the smaller size gives better navigation and readability than a broadsheet, but at the same time the page size does not affect the quality of journalism by imposing space constraints in the way the compact tabloid format does. As for layout, while broadsheets and Berliners favour text over images and graphics, and display several stories on the same page, in compacts visual effects dominate – compact pages are characterized by big headlines (story titles), a variety of typefaces and printed symbols, large photographs, few columns of text and short articles.

The different preferences in design of broadsheets, tabloids and Berliners can be seen in Figure 4.1, comparing the front pages of three British national newspapers. The first is from the *Daily Telegraph*, one of the few surviving broadsheets in London; the second is from the *Guardian*, a Berliner and one of the best-selling UK dailies; the third is from the *Daily Mirror*, a tabloid. Together, these front pages illustrate differences that result from catering for different readerships.

The *Daily Telegraph* targets a traditional, conservative audience. It uses the most conservative format and a 7-column-grid design (see section 4.5), with the main picture in the centre, and the text occupying a large portion of the front page. In this issue three stories are covered in the page, each being allotted a separate section and separated from the other sections by a solid line. A horizontal line separates the articles from the advertisement positioned at the bottom of the page. Different font sizes and types are used in the headlines, only some of them being in bold. Above the nameplate (the title of the publication), space is left for more leisure information: spreading across the top of the page, from left to right, are a promo, with a picture, and the headlines (in red) and sub-heads of two feature stories, one of them with a picture headshot; below each is a jumpline (the line that tells the reader on which page the story can be found), to invite readers to search inside the paper.

The page of the *Guardian* is structured on a 5-column grid, which allows larger fonts and greater legibility than the 7-column grid of the *Daily*

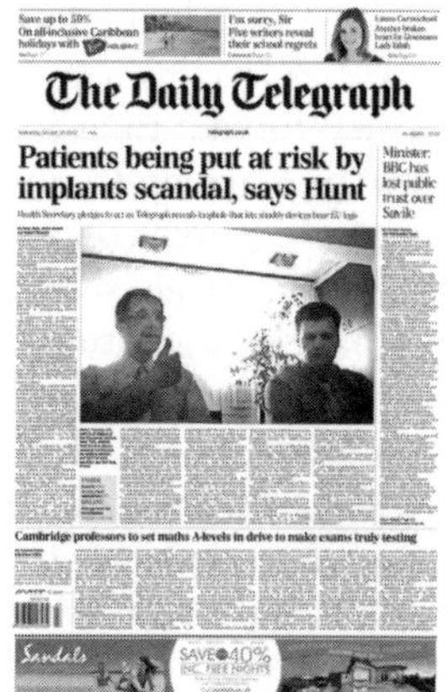

The Daily Telegraph

Patients being put at risk by implants scandal, says Hunt

Minister: BBC has lost public trust over Savile

Cambridge professors to set maths A-levels in drive to make exams truly testing

Sandals SAVE 40%

US travel special

Javier Bardem

PLUS 25% OFF

theguardian

weekend edition

Savile scandal: now Whitehall is dragged in

I can't understand it · in Greece we are experiencing war

DAILY Mirror

EXCLUSIVE

AT LAST! HOOK'S GONE

Cheryl

MISSING GIRL MURDER PROBE

I SAW APRIL DRIVEN OFF

Witness says he was the last to see her alive

Town's tears as cops now search for body

Figure 4.1 Differences in front-page design in three UK newspapers using different formats. Left to right: the *Daily Telegraph*[1] (broadsheet), the *Guardian*[2] (Berliner), and the *Daily Mirror*[3] (tabloid).

Telegraph. In the top section of the page, above the nameplate, a considerable prominence is given to the colour advertisement that occupies about 20% of the whole page. This coloured band highlights stories inside the paper, as well as an offer from the *Guardian*'s mail-order bookshop. The use of colour in this section increases the visual impact of the paper while attracting readers' attention to some feature stories inside that are considered particularly noteworthy. In this issue, the front page focuses on three news stories. The main one, appearing on the left of the page below a large-font headline, is about one of Britain's biggest stars, the late Jimmy Savile, being involved in a sex scandal. With two columns of text on the front page, a substantial part of this news story is told up-front, allowing the reader to access much of it without having to turn the page. Alongside this text, separated by a vertical line, is a big picture of the woman at the centre of the second story: a Russian singer released on probation after being sentenced for hooliganism. There is no text for this story, except for the picture caption (see section 4.5). The reader is directed to page 23 of the paper to read the full text. A solid horizontal line separates the main, upper portion of the page from the lower portion. Below the line the third story in focus is a piece by the newspaper's correspondent in Greece, Helena Smith, commenting on the award of the Nobel Prize for peace to the EU at a time when the economic situation in Greece makes it feel as if the country is at war. A headshot of the correspondent is shown next to the text. Finally, at the far-right of the page, a series of boxes with smaller images and coloured headlines directs readers' attention to comment articles and features in different sections of the paper, to help the reader navigate inside the paper; in the bottom-right corner there is an advertisement. The same font is used throughout the page, though it varies in size, emboldening and colour, in a style that is modern and approachable.

The *Daily Mirror* front page has a much stronger visual impact than the other two. This is achieved through the use of colours, pictures and large type sizes, which dominate the page; the news story proper occupies only a small portion of it, and there are no advertisements. The page shows close-ups of the people whose stories are told in the paper, suggesting a focus on the human subjects. The language is colloquial and emotional, and the appeal is emphasized by the use of characters in bold and colour, which is meant to help capture the readers' attention. The nameplate appears on a red background at the top of the page, following the British tradition of the so-called 'red-tops' or 'pops' tabloids. Below and at the right of the nameplate are three headshots, with headlines and jumplines (see section 4.5) referring the readers to stories to be found on later pages. The front page is centred on one news story, which is introduced by a very big headline, in bold and upper case, and set to justified margins. The text of the headline synthesizes the dramatic content of the story, dealing with the disappearance of a little girl; the byline (see section 4.5) and the first paragraph of the story are in bold, following another convention of tabloids. Bold type in a larger type size make the lead (the first paragraph) of the story very prominent. It is followed by a couple of paragraphs, and then the story is continued on another page. The *Daily Mirror* also differs from the *Guardian* and the *Daily Telegraph* in the kinds of stories that are considered newsworthy. It gives great relevance to a story that occurred within the UK – about the little girl who disappeared after she was driven off in a stranger's car. This front page carries no mention of political or economic issues, or international affairs. As is typical of tabloids, the focus of the paper is on human-interest stories. This reflects the paper's desire to appeal to a more 'popular' audience than those of the *Guardian* and the *Daily Telegraph*, which are aimed at higher social groupings and contain more stories focusing on politics, economics, and international events.

4.4 Redesigning a paper

To meet their readers' demands, to keep up with changes in technology, and also to improve the usability and effectiveness of advertising, from time to time newspapers redesign their print editions. A form of redesign that has become common internationally since the early 2000s involves reducing the newspaper size. This is aimed at attracting younger readerships, making papers easier to read (especially on public transport) and saving costs. The tendency has been to switch from the broadsheet format to the compact format, or to the Berliner. As a result, many countries, like Australia, Canada and the UK, no longer consider broadsheets the only suitable format for delivering in-depth stories, and the compact (or tabloid) format is becoming popular in many Asian countries, including China. In Europe many newspapers have adopted the Berliner, a format also adopted by various papers in South America. On the other hand, in countries like India and the US the broadsheet is still considered the traditional and suitable format for the dissemination of printed news.

Redesigning a paper does not simply mean changing its format, but also changing some of the conventions used in the layout. Such changes often involve the nameplate, the column grid design, the size of images in the page and the size of headlines. The trend is towards greater visual impact through the use of larger headlines and more colour. Colour is used to call attention to certain textual and visual elements, as well as to make the page more pleasing to the eye. Relying more on pictures and less on text to convey content meets the needs of present-day users accustomed to assimilating visual information and watching sophisticated videos, and it better suits people without the time to read long stories. In this sense, comparing the front pages of the *Daily Telegraph* and the *Guardian* in Figure 4.1, the latter appears more innovative than the former, because it presents a higher percentage of visual (rather than textual) information.

4.5 Meaning through a multimodal layout

As we saw in Chapter 2, in media texts, visual and non-verbal elements (photographs, videos, diagrams and graphics) are integrated with verbal elements (spoken or written words). In both online and print news, all elements of the design work in conjunction to create meaning and provide readers with a clear interpretative framework to navigate through the publication. In any given paper's design the combination of elements creates a style that matches what readers expect of that paper.

The most important element of design is the **layout**, which conveys valuable information on the relative importance of the stories and so aids their comprehension. For both print and online newspapers, position in the page conveys information about a story's news relevance, with higher and more central texts more relevant than lower and less central pieces. In addition, texts are organized in modular fashion: each module is divided from the next by a white border or subtle line, so that readers can easily connect photographs, images, charts, etc., to their related stories. Different thematic sections (for example, international news, local news, politics, sports, entertainment, business, etc.) help readers find the information they are looking for.

Because graphic and visual elements are easier and faster to grasp than verbal information, pictures and images – together with typological devices, such as big headlines, figure captions (see below), differences of type size and font, fact boxes and charts – are used to give readers some basic information on the news content as soon as their eyes hit the page. Colour may be used to highlight and emphasize, also helping the interpretation of texts. Stories that sacrifice some text in favour of pictures are usually preferred to long-story texts. Nevertheless, pages typically alternate between stories with longer and shorter texts to offer readers more variety.

The **nameplate** (the title and logo of the publication) is obviously one of the most important elements of the design, as this is what carries the brand of the newspaper. It is placed at the top of the front page (or home page) in both print and online newspapers.

Headlines (story titles) fulfil the critical function of attracting the readers' attention. Through their size and positioning in the page, they also signal the relative importance of the text with respect to other stories; news with bigger headlines placed in the centre-top position in the page being more relevant than that with smaller headlines placed more peripherally. Like all other aspects of design, the type fonts used in the headlines and texts are chosen for their anticipated effect on the reader. As we have already seen, in general broadsheets differ from tabloids in having a less strong visual impact and in using smaller characters, less bold type and less colloquial, emotional language.

Pictures, too, are used in news reporting to attract the reader's attention, and to enhance the story. They are selected to emphasize the particular approach the story takes, often by showing vivid details that complement the verbal narration of the events. Photographs can now be manipulated

Bedford charter flight co. to touch down at 2 airports

y IRA KANTOR

Worcester Regional Airport gets a boost today as Rectrix Aviation, which operates private charter flights, begins construction of a new facility there to fuel, de-ice and service planes.

The Bedford-based company actually kicks off work at two fixed-base operator facilities today — a 60,000 square feet building at Hanscom Field and another totaling 22,000 square feet at the nearly deserted Worcester ai[illegible]rt — that will create between 85 a[illegible] new jobs, Rectrix CEO Rich Cawley [illegible] the Herald.

"The hockey stick growth in front of us is tremendous," he said. "A lot of companies based in Massachusetts are ... heading out towards Worcester. The timing is perfect for us."

The company is investing $20 million in both FBOs, which will provide light maintenance, fueling and de-icing services for airlines, after winning a Massachusetts Port Authority contract earlier this year.

Rectrix currently has four planes at its disposal, and FBOs at Hyannis and Sarasota, Fla., airports. The company expects to have the new facilities complete by next spring.

RICH CAWLEY

With orders in for 10 to 15 more planes over the next two to three years, the private air charter hopes to offer commercial passenger service at Barnstable Municipal Airport and Worcester Regional Airport in the future, with destinations including New York, Florida and the Midwest, Cawley said.

The company said it needs to first apply for a certificate from the Federal Aviation Administration that allows it to sell tickets on a per-seat basis to the public, and secure air slots at various airports.

"Right now there's not a lot of aircraft available to legacy carriers," Cawley said. "When those aircraft become available, that's when you see expansion really spike up."

Worcester Regional Airport Director Andrew Davis said it costs $5 million each year — or nearly $14,000 a day — to operate the Massport-owned airport, which has had no scheduled air service since the departure of Direct Air earlier this year.

"We would love to see it," Davis said. "Having Rectrix being there enhances our focus on providing commercial air service, benefits central Massachusetts, and turns more attention to other carriers to take a closer look at (the airport)."

The agency has been in constant communication with several airline carriers, including JetBlue, about touching down at the airport.

— ira.kantor@bostonherald.com

BOOST: Empty Worcester Regional Airport, left and below, will soon get a Rectrix Aviation fixed-base operations facility.

STAFF FILE PHOTOS BY STUART CAHILL

BOS[illegible]ERALD THURSDAY, NOVEMBER 1, 2012

Figure 4.2 Terms used in a newspaper page.[4]

easily – by cropping, scaling, retouching – which gives journalists another way to control the emphasis of a story. In tabloids the pictures tend to match the sensationalist tone of the language and create a strong visual impact, showing close-ups, details, etc. In broadsheets pictures are smaller and generally more discreet.

Captions, the short texts found next to an image, are used to provide a link between the text and the image, which is important because the meaning conveyed by images is less direct than that conveyed by language, and pictures may be ambiguous. Captions may contain the name of the person the news story is about, or a brief description of the event described. For captions, small type sizes are used, and the font may be different from that of the body copy.

The choice of **typeface**, or font (the set of letters and other characters of a common design used in the texts) represents a subtle tool for reporters to convey meaning. Newspapers may use different fonts to suggest different approaches to the text (e.g., more or less modern) or to create a variation that has the effect of capturing the reader's attention. Typically, fonts of different sizes are used to suit different situations, or to contrast the relevance of stories appearing on the same page. Bigger, bold characters are used in headlines. The characters used in front-page headlines may be especially large when the news is deemed really extraordinary, as, for example, with major natural events such as devastating tsunamis, earthquakes, etc.

Figure 4.2 illustrates the elements of a page layout using an inside page from the *Boston Herald.*

On the print newspaper page, space is distributed in a column format, according to predetermined grids. **Grids** give structure to a design by allowing texts to be arranged in columns on the page. An example of a 5-column grid is given in Figure 4.3.

Grid structures ensure that the newspaper content is shaped into proportions that are pleasing and processable by the eye. The choice of grids affects the readers' reading 'rhythm'. This will be slowed down by wide column grids and speeded up by narrow ones; hence the former are used for 'weighty statements', while the latter are more appropriate for a 'snappy, business-like' style of news.

Most newspapers use a variety of grids in different pages. In general, broadsheets use a 6-column grid, especially on inside pages, where ads are sold in standard widths that require columns about 11 or 12 picas wide.[5] Variations may include half-column grids, or grids within grids, as in Figure 4.3. On front pages a variety of grids may be used. Tabloids use most commonly the 4- or 5-column grid, where text can be more comfortably distributed across the page. The front pages in Figure 4.1 in section 4.3 show examples of a 7-column, a 5-column and a 4-column grid format, respectively from the *Daily Telegraph*, the *Guardian* and the *Daily Mirror*.

Figure 4.3 An example of a 5-column grid.

4.6 Designing multimodal news for the web

Design is as important for online news as for print news. For both, good design is essential to ensuring the product's attractiveness to the audience and its readability and success. In online news, just as in print news, all elements in the design work in conjunction with language to create meaning and provide readers with a clear interpretative framework to navigate through the publication.

Clearly, design is approached differently in online news, due to the difference in medium and the way in which texts are created and read off the web. However, many agencies issuing both print and online news model their electronic pages after the print layout, so that there is a high level of resemblance between the two versions. For example, traditional newspapers that also have a presence online tend to create an online nameplate with characteristics similar to their print ones. There is in fact a conceptual continuity between traditional and online newspapers that is synthesized in the expression 'newspaper metaphor' (Ihlström and Lundberg, 2003); it can be seen by comparing the front pages in Figure 4.1 with those at the following addresses: www.telegraph.co.uk; www.guardian.co.uk; www. mirror.co.uk.

As with print news design, online news design is aimed at helping readers navigate through the news content. One of the most common navigation styles is the *tabloid*, which reproduces the traditional newspaper layout of the same name. With this style, the screen is divided into sections, each containing a number of topic links for the reader to choose from. The purpose is to provide a lot of options up-front, so as to attract a wide variety of audiences and direct them to the information of interest. Typically, the front page contains all the news story headlines, linked to the full article. Headlines are arranged either vertically or horizontally, with the more newsworthy stories in the upper part of the screen, followed by the lead and a picture. Advertisements, in different sizes and multimedia formats, tend to be placed on the right side of the page. Examples of websites using the tabloid navigation format are: USA Today (www.usatoday.com); MSNBC (www.msnbc.com); CNN (www.cnn.com).

Unlike print newspapers, where traditional editorial practice involves daily changes in the layout of the front page, online papers tend to maintain the same front-page layout in different editions. This is because web pages are based on a fixed design that allows fast updates of content but requires more work for changes in layout – and, considering the number of times a day an online paper is updated, such work is impractical.

In addition, given the limited visual area of the screen, very large headlines and pictures are not favoured in online news, as they reduce the amount of information that can be shown on the front page. Instead websites aim to present a lot of options for links up-front, to increase their attractiveness for the audience. Rather than opting for large characters and pictures, they prefer eye-catching design that can be easily implemented by supplementing the page layout with illustrative material, boxes, colour, different font sizes and types, etc. However, rapid changes in digital technology, leading to modifications in software and the user interface to websites, may bring about substantial alterations in the navigation styles considered appropriate for creating and reading news online.

Students' activities

Activity 1

Access a site where today's newspaper front pages are shown (for example: www.frontpagestoday.co.uk; www.newseum.org). Then access a site where you can find archived front pages from the past (for example, the British Library shows over twenty at: www.bl.uk/onlinegallery/features/frontpage/universe.html). Compare and contrast today's pages with older ones. How has newspaper design changed over time? What changes have occurred with regard to text, visuals and white space over the years? What are the current trends by which we may establish criteria to evaluate the attractiveness of a newspaper?

Activity 2

Accessing www.frontpagestoday.co.uk or www.newseum.org, find two papers from the same country that, from what you can tell by looking at their front pages, target the same kind of readership. Analyse how the two papers give prominence to different news, and how this is reflected in their design.

Activity 3

Tabloids have a long and well-established tradition in Britain. Tabloids exist in the US too, but their characteristics differ somewhat from British tabloids. Comparing the front pages of the US tabloids in Figure 2.2 with that of the British tabloid in Figure 4.1, what differences in design and/or language do you observe? If you need more examples, use the front pages retrievable at: www.frontpagestoday.co.uk/.

Activity 4

Words have a literal or primary meaning (the first meaning of the word given in the dictionary when you look it up), and an associated or secondary meaning, given by the emotions and associations that particular words carry. The first meaning is referred to as **denotation**, the second as **connotation**.

Words can have positive, negative or neutral connotations. Words like *chair* or *school* tend to have a neutral connotation. Here are some examples of words with positive or negative connotations:

difficult (negative)	challenging (positive)
stingy (negative)	economical (positive)
headstrong (negative)	determined (positive)
nit picking (negative)	meticulous (positive)
astute (negative)	sagacious (positive)
childish (negative)	childlike (positive)

Because even synonyms of the same word vary in their connotations, when reading news it is important to consider every word a reporter chooses, to determine whether a word may provide a slant to the interpretation of the text.

Below are groups of words that are often used to describe people. Can you tell if they have a positive or negative connotation?

1 Youthful, Young, Immature, Juvenile
2 Disabled, Crippled
3 Relaxed, Laid-back, Easy-going

4 Slim, Skinny, Slender, Thin
5 Cheap, Frugal, Miserly, Economical
6 Inquisitive, Interested, Curious, Convivial
7 Confident, Secure, Proud, Egotistical
8 Lovely, Knockout, Beautiful, Stunning
9 Talkative, Conversational, Chatty, Nosy

Further reading

Adam, G.S., and Adam, P.S. 2002. 'Writing, editing, design', in R.P. Clark and C.C. Campbell (eds), *The Values and Craft of American Journalism: Essays from the Poynter Institute*, Gainsville, University Press of Florida, 133–47.

Adam, P.S. 2000. 'How W.E.D. works', www.poynter.org/content/content_view.asp?id=4553.

BrassTacksDesign: www.brasstacksdesign.com/design.htm.

Durant, A., and Lambrou, M. 2009. *Language and Media: A Resource Book for Students*, London and New York, Routledge.

Lorusso, A.M., and Violi, P. 2004. *Semiotica del Testo Giornalistico*, Rome and Bari, Laterza.

Lynch, P.J., and Horton, S. 2009. *Web Style Guide: Basic Design Principles for Creating Web Sites*, 3rd ed., New Haven CT and London, Yale University Press.

Machin, D., and Niblock, S. 2006. *News Production: Theory and Practice*, London and New York, Routledge.

Morton, J. 2005. 'Bye, bye broadsheet?', *American Journalism Review*, June/July 2005, www.ajr.org/article.asp?id=3904.

Nel, F. 2005. *Writing for the Media in Southern Africa*, 3rd ed., Cape Town, Oxford University Press.

Rudin, R., and Ibbotson, T. 2002. *An Introduction to Journalism*, Oxford, Focal Press.

Van Wagener, A., 2003. 'The grid: the structure of design', www.poynter.org/how-tos/newsgathering-storytelling/visual-voice/12369/the-grid-the-structure-of-design.

Chapter 5

Structuring the story

Three basic features characterize the news story: story structure, impersonal language and coherent texts. Here we examine the most commonly used types of news story structures, including the 'Inverted Pyramid', the Hourglass, and narrative story-telling. Then we look at how journalists need to use impersonal language to maintain an objective tone, but can convey their opinions through their selection of their sources' words and the order of presentation of the events. Finally, we consider the strategies used to logically link the paragraphs in a story.

5.1 Basic story structures

News stories tend to follow one of a series of set structures for their exposition and development, starting with the headline, progressing to the lead and developing onwards from there. Several structures are available that help reporters shape the story into a logical, well-organized unit that can be understood by the reader. A basic principle is to identify the urgent, the essential, and provide a simple, clear, depersonalized and sober account of the events. However, in most cases, the type of story to be told will determine the type of structure chosen to tell it. The following sections discuss some of the structures used by journalists to write their stories.

5.2 The Inverted Pyramid

The most basic news story form, and the one that best expresses the element of urgency in reporting, is the so-called 'Inverted Pyramid'. This is commonly used for hard news. It is based on the idea that the elements of a story should be arranged in decreasing order of importance, with the most important ones appearing at the top, and the less important – for example, background information – following below. This reverses the chronological order and gradual build-up to the conclusion that is typical of narrative style: the conclusion of the story comes at the outset, followed by other crucial information, with less important information found at the end of the article.

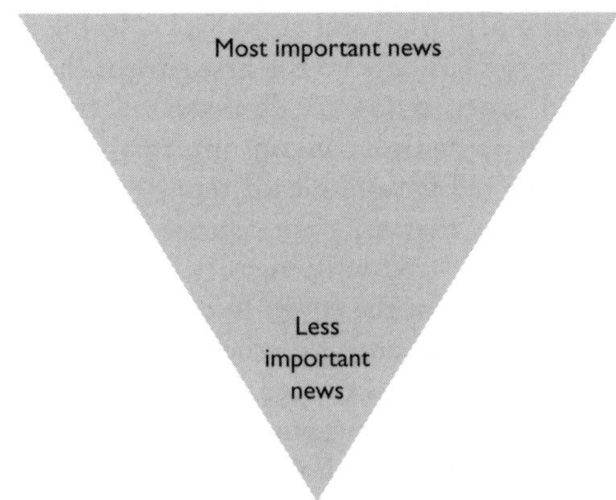

Figure 5.1 A schematic representation of the Inverted Pyramid story structure.

The Inverted Pyramid is the most traditional story form. Its origins are unclear, but it is likely to have evolved during the American Civil War (1861–5), when stories were transmitted over telegraph wires, as part of a strategy to ensure that editors would get the story endings notwithstanding any truncations of the communication transmissions. It is also possible that it evolved simply to meet our society's need for the fast delivery of information.

There are several reasons why, despite much criticism of it (see below), the Inverted Pyramid is still the most commonly used structure for presenting hard news. One of its advantages is that it allows readers to assimilate the crucial elements of the story quickly and clearly, so that they can swiftly decide whether they want to continue reading it or not. This is valuable in today's fast-paced life, because readers may only have a limited time to read newspapers – research shows that the average time spent reading a paper is about 25 minutes.[1]

The structure also serves the needs of the newspaper editors. To fit them into the assigned space on the page, Inverted Pyramid stories can be trimmed from the bottom without any significant loss of information. For online news, the Inverted Pyramid style suits the reading pattern of the impatient web-user who prefers to scan online texts rather than read them; also, since the important information appears in the top portion of the screen, it is not necessary for readers to scroll down. Finally, the Inverted Pyramid facilitates daily updates of online stories by allowing editors to add new information to the top part of the article and leave the information at the bottom unaltered.

As for reporters, the Inverted Pyramid forces them to identify and rank the most important elements in the narration, and use a fast-flowing style of writing, delaying or avoiding altogether the recounting of minor details. Overall, this is considered to be a very good structure for summarizing and delivering news information quickly and effectively.

On the other hand, it also has some drawbacks. In the first place, it does not encourage readers to read beyond the first part of the article: interest in an Inverted Pyramid story tends to diminish as the story progresses, because each successive paragraph contains information of less importance. Secondly, while the Inverted Pyramid leads reporters to use their best skills to write article beginnings that are very concise and effective, it does not encourage them to compose well-written story endings or to give the same news value to all paragraphs of the story. In other words, it may lead them to oversimplify the writing and creative process.

Because of its drawbacks, the Inverted Pyramid is much criticized, and many newspaper editors encourage reporters to adopt new writing forms to increase the appeal of stories and to hold the readers' attention. A common variation of the Inverted Pyramid consists of a series of smaller Inverted Pyramids, each designed to summarize a part of the story, provide details, background information, description and comments. At the bottom tip of each pyramid is a turn: a clause or sentence designed to engage the readers and push them forward to the next bit of information.

For all its limitations, the Inverted Pyramid remains the favourite form for many news stories, because it is still the best possible format for delivering fast, effective and clear news. With the spread of information services delivered via mobile devices, which convey news in very condensed formats, its popularity seems to be on the rise.

5.2.1 An example of an Inverted Pyramid story

The story below, reporting on a body found in a house in Castro Valley, California, is written with an Inverted Pyramid structure.

Body found in burning Castro Valley home[2]

(Henry K. Lee, www.sfgate.com, October 18, 2012)

1 A woman's body was found early Thursday after firefighters doused a suspicious blaze at a Castro Valley home belonging to a retired male San Francisco firefighter, authorities and neighbours said.

2 The fire was reported at a home on the 2400 block of San Carlos Avenue about 12:15 a.m. Alameda County firefighters quickly put out the fire and found the body after searching the residence, authorities said.

3 The dead woman's name has not been released. A coroner's autopsy will determine what killed her.

4 Sheriff's Sgt. J.D. Nelson said it appeared an accelerant may have been used to start the fire. He said he did not know if investigators had been able to contact the home's owner.

5 Authorities waited to obtain a search warrant before inspecting the residence, Nelson said.

6 He said it was too early to determine if the death was the result of an accident or a homicide.
7 Investigators have also not ruled out the possibility of suicide, Nelson said, noting that there have been cases in which people trying to kill themselves have used accelerant to start fires.
8 'We're going to pull out all the stops to make sure what we're doing is correct and, if in fact this was a homicide, that we have the upper hand on it,' Nelson said.
9 The home belongs to Michael Rice, 60, who served in the San Francisco Fire Department for 27 years before he retired as a lieutenant in 2009, said department spokeswoman Mindy Talmadge.
10 Laurie Iniguez, 32, a next-door neighbour, said Rice lives at the home with his girlfriend.
11 'It's definitely unnerving,' Iniguez said. 'We're just sending up prayers, hoping that our worst suspicions aren't confirmed.'
12 Another acquaintance of the couple told reporters that Rice was on vacation in Utah.

The headline presents a condensed summary of the story, introducing the basic information of the reported event. This basic information is then expanded in the lead (paragraph 1), which provides a brief summary of the story, and introduces the *who*, *what*, *where* and *how* of the reported event, following the conventions of journalism. Paragraph 2 expands on the lead and provides a more detailed description of the facts leading to the conclusion of the story: i.e., the finding of the body. Paragraph 3 adds detail to the finding of the body reported in the previous paragraph. Paragraphs 4–7 report a series of quotes from Sheriff Sgt. J.D. Nelson, the main source of the story, who mentions possible hypotheses and opinions about the causes of the woman's death. Paragraph 9 provides some information about the owner of the house where the body was found. The last three paragraphs complement the story, but the information they contain only marginally amplifies the reported event, and removing it would not fundamentally affect the structure of the story.

5.3 The Hourglass

The Hourglass, a story form that has become rather popular in recent years, combines elements of both Inverted Pyramid and traditional storytelling. The main facts are told in the first paragraphs of the story, presented in order of decreasing importance, as in an Inverted Pyramid. In the second part of the story the events are then narrated in chronological order, and space is left for detail, dialogue and background information. The chronological narration of the events is usually introduced by a turn, or transition, which provides overall attribution for the following narrative.

Since attribution is given in this transition, the writer does not thereafter need to attribute every sentence of the narrated events. Examples of transitional paragraphs are: *Police gave the following account of the accident..., The victim told the jury what happened..., Johnson said that he was attacked shortly after he left work* ... (from Itule and Anderson, 2007: 71). A schematic representation of the Hourglass style is shown in Figure 5.2.

The Hourglass structure works well with police stories, dramatic events such as disasters, trials, or any other story that lends itself to chronological narration. Its advantage is that, while readers can still get the basic facts quickly, the story is made more dramatic by the narrative style, and benefits from having a balanced structure and a real ending. That real ending gives readers an incentive to read the article right through and 'discourages editors from slashing from the bottom' (Itule and Anderson, 2007: 72). A disadvantage of this format is that some information appearing at the top of the story may be repeated in the chronological portion, making the story longer than the Inverted Pyramid.

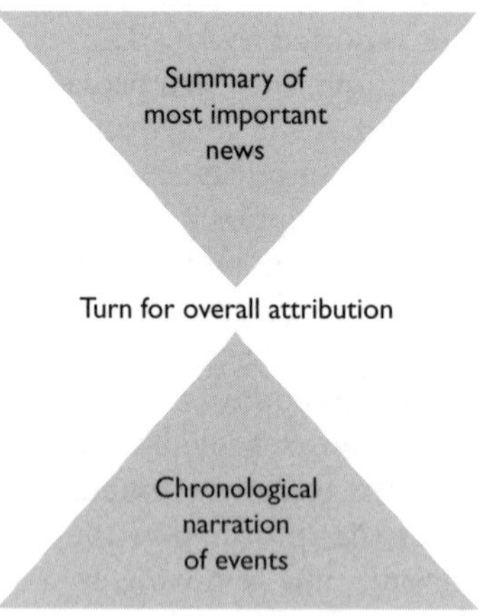

Figure 5.2 A schematic representation of the Hourglass story structure.

5.3.1 *An example of an Hourglass story*

The article below is written with an Hourglass structure, telling the story of two young men arrested for selling drugs.

> **Wilson High School student, 17, and man, 18, sold Ecstasy to undercover detective, police say**[3]
> He and man, 18, sold Ecstasy, police say
> (Steven Henshaw, readingeagle.com, May 14, 2009)

1 A 17-year-old Wilson High School student and an 18-year-old man were arrested after they sold Ecstasy to an undercover Spring Township detective for a third time, police said Wednesday.
2 The student and Daniel Urdaneta-Gomez sold 30 Ecstasy pills for $390 after arranging by text message to meet the detective Tuesday night in a shopping center parking lot, police said.
3 Police withheld the student's name because he was charged as a juvenile. They said he lives in the township.
4 He is in the Berks County Youth Center awaiting a hearing on charges of possessing and delivering a controlled substance, conspiracy and intending to use drug paraphernalia.
5 Urdaneta-Gomez of the 600 block of Vester Place, Sinking Spring, was arraigned on the same charges before Senior District Judge Richard A. Gatti and committed to the county prison in lieu of $20,000 bail.
6 Police gave this account:
7 Detectives learned in April that the 17-year-old was selling marijuana and Ecstasy pills in the West Lawn area.
8 The undercover detective obtained the student's cell phone number and exchanged several text messages with him. They agreed to meet April 22 in the parking lot.
9 The student parked his car next to the detective's car and Urdaneta-Gomez got into it.
10 Urdaneta-Gomez told the detective he could get him as many pills as he wanted for $15 a pill.
11 But Urdaneta-Gomez said he didn't have all the pills the detective wanted, so he sold him a sample for $10.
12 The detective asked if he had any marijuana, and Urdaneta-Gomez sold him five small bags for $60.
13 The detective bought 30 Ecstasy pills from the two on April 28 for $400 and on Tuesday night for $390.
14 Police got a search warrant and found a small amount of marijuana and paraphernalia in the student's car.

The basic story facts are introduced in the headline and synthesized in the lead: A 17-year-old Wilson High School student and an 18-year-old man were arrested after they sold Ecstasy to an undercover Spring Township detective for a third time, police said Wednesday. Paragraph 2 expands on the lead by providing all the story details, such as the name and age of the man who was selling the drug with the student; the number and price of the pills the two were selling; how they arranged to meet the detective; and the time and place the event occurred. In other words, this paragraph provides the *who*, *what*, *how*, *when* and *where* of the story. Paragraphs 3 and 4 give details of what happened to the two after the arrest. The turn comes in paragraph 6: *Police gave this account*. After the turn, the story is told again in a narrative style – facts are told in chronological order, with richness of detail, yielding a better description of how events actually evolved.

5.4 Narrative story-telling

In recent years, online media organizations and agencies have been exploring new ways to make news-story reading more appealing to their readership, so as to increase their audiences and their advertising revenue. Particularly online, journalists are exploring new writing styles and formats to overcome the limitations of the traditional Inverted Pyramid and give readers a more enjoyable reading experience. Because of the virtually unlimited size of the web page, conciseness is no longer fundamental to news writing, and journalists can venture into less compact styles, which are also more readable off the screen. Some of these changes can be seen in the so-called narrative style of journalism, or narrative story-telling.

The origins of narrative story-telling in journalism can be traced back to the period after the American Civil War, when, to convey the pain and suffering caused by the war, journalists felt the need to lessen the distance between the observer and the observed. This style was then overshadowed in mainstream journalism until revitalized with the birth of New Journalism in the 1960s, and has enjoyed renewed success over the past forty years.

At the core of narrative story-telling is the idea that true-life stories should be written using the codes and conventions of narrative, rather than those of journalism. Narratives are common in our daily life, as they represent one way of recounting past events. They are used in a broad range of human activities, and can take many forms, including anecdotes, fairy tales, jokes, comics, novels, etc. Narratives draw upon the basic human capacity to transfer experience from one person to another, and it is for this reason that the media 'package' real events and characters into stories (film dramas, documentaries, soap operas, advertisements) that are of public interest and can be presented to an audience.

The process of story-creation involves some key elements:

- a narrator, who organizes, selects and recounts the events and characters within the narrative, as well as providing the point of view from which the action and characters are presented;
- a listener or an audience (real or implied) to tell the stories to;
- a structure of presentation of the events, which are often told in chronological order (from beginning to end).

Typically, narratives share a core structure: they present an initial state of order that is in some way disturbed, and action needs to be taken to re-establish the equilibrium. This basic structure has been given various formalizations by different researchers. An influential model of narratives (Labov 1997, based on Labov and Waletzky 1967) recognizes a six-stage structure that includes: an *abstract*, which signals what the story is about; an *orientation,* which gives information on the time and place of the events, on the identities of the participants and their initial behaviour; a *complicating action* which creates the problem or disorder (the turning point) that will require a response and involve further action; an *evaluation* which highlights what the consequences of the event are for human needs and desires; a *resolution* and/or a *coda*, which return the narrative to the initial state and time, and may contain a moral. Narratives are also characterized by the frequent use of first-person pronouns, especially if recounting first-person experiences, the use of the past tense, descriptive and emotional language, and the presence of concrete and specific details.

In narrative story-telling, unlike the Inverted Pyramid, stories do not contain a lead in the traditional sense and do not present information in decreasing order of importance. Generally, the first paragraphs set the scene – often a description of the situation or place where the event occurred; they do not provide detailed contextual information, including a summary and outcomes of events, thus inviting the audience to read on. Events are narrated in chronological order, following the traditional scheme of beginning, middle and end, and build to a final 'climax'. People are prominent, and their actions are portrayed vividly and with details. The sources are described as real characters that live the events being reported. Dialogue is often used to increase the vividness and effectiveness of the story, which appears to be developing before the reader's eyes. Other features include personal voice (as opposed to the impersonality advocated by traditional journalism), and 'robust' language, which uses tone, colour, rhythm and alliteration to reveal nuances, describe people, places and events, and create engaging texts. Narration resembles the style used in novels more than in hard news stories. However, unlike novels, narrative news stories are documented and based on actual facts.

Story-telling is suitable for the main feature stories, but is also widely adopted for stories that may have a high emotional impact on the audience, such as crime and court stories. The use of this story structure is increasingly being encouraged, especially in online news, because it aids reading news by presenting it in a way that is involving and appealing for the reader. This structure is favoured by broadcast media, which prefer the traditional chronological narrative structure over the Inverted Pyramid, as it is more compatible with the oral presentation of events.

5.4.1 An example of a narrative story-telling style

The article reported below is written in a narrative story-telling style. It deals with a car bombing in Baghdad's oldest book market, in which many people were killed or injured and the market destroyed.

> **Anguish in the Ruins of Mutanabi Street**[4]
> In Baghdad's Literary District, Mourning Loved Ones and a Once-Unifying Place
>
> (Sudarsan Raghavan, Washington Post Foreign Service, March 10, 2007)

1 BAGHDAD, March 9 – On a pile of bricks, someone had left a pink plastic flower, a pair of glasses and a book with crisp, white pages. They glowed in the black debris of Mutanabi Street, which by Friday had become a graveyard of memories. At 9:03 a.m., a man in a rumpled brown suit walked past dark banners mourning the dead. He stopped near the flower and the book, which was opened to a chapter on the virtues of Baghdad.

2 'There is no God but God,' he said, his voice disappearing in the cracking sound of a shovel against debris. He stared at the gutted bookshops, hollowed like skulls by the blast and the flames. He lowered his head, fighting back tears.

3 Then he turned and walked away.

4 On Friday morning, Iraqis continued to drift to Mutanabi Street, four days after a car bomb took the lives of at least 26 people and injured dozens more. Some came to hunt for the remains of loved ones. Others came to mourn a street that represented the intellectual soul of a nation known for its love affair with books. For many, the narrow warren of shops had seemed to defy Iraq's woes.

5 Mutanabi Street had long been considered 'the unifier of Iraq,' said Khalid Hussein, a bookseller with cropped hair and thick forearms. Before the bombing, he said, this was 'the only place that hadn't been touched by sectarianism'.

6 The evidence was lodged in the dense heaps of twisted metal and the mangled cars. Here, a page from a Bible. There, a page from a Koran. Tattered posters of Imam Ali, Shiite Islam's revered saint, littered the ground near the 8-foot-wide crater left by the bomb. The shop that sold Wahhabi Sunni literature was in ruins.

7 The day after the attack, blackened body parts covered with cardboard and pink stationery sat near a storefront. A note read: 'The remains of Hadi Hassan. Hummus seller.' He was a Shiite from Najaf, said those who knew him.

8 A few inches away, a dusty, charred cellphone lay next to an empty yellow plastic bag and a shard of burned flesh stuck to cloth. A note read: 'This is the only remains from this person. Everyone is going back to God.'

9 By Friday, the body parts had vanished. Around Khalid Hussein were fathers and sons, strangers and friends. The smells of smoke and burned paper lingered. Scavengers looked for loot, but nobody paid attention.

10 'This is his shoe,' a man cried out. 'I bought it for him.'

11 It was 9:06 a.m. The man was slim, with peppery hair and square, gray-tinted glasses. He clutched a black chunk of flat leather melted by the heat. 'I bought it for him.'

12 He kissed the piece of leather, then placed it gently on a warped metal box next to the flower, the eyeglasses and the book.

13 'Come and see it,' he yelled to five men delicately digging through debris. 'It is his size.' He broke into tears.

14 'This is your shoe,' he yelled, looking toward the pale blue sky. 'My son, I bought it for you.'

15 He fell to his knees, sobbing.

16 The six men, all relatives, were hunting for a teenager's remains. The boy had been shopping for notebooks on Mutanabi Street, named for a 10th-century poet. They had been digging since Wednesday, morning till evening.

17 They stared blankly at the shoe. No one had the heart to tell the father the truth.

18 So they kept digging.

19 'Don't step hard,' the father said. 'Don't harm him.'

20 At 9:15 a.m., Najah al-Hayawi, short with gray hair and a white mustache, emerged with his son from a building with smoke-covered Grecian pillars. The car bomb had exploded in front of their family's Renaissance bookstore, one of the street's oldest.

21 'We've been here since 1957,' Hayawi lamented.

22 Hayawi's brother Mohammad, a burly Sunni Arab with twinkling honey-colored eyes, was killed. So was his nephew, the only son of another brother, Nabil. Nabil, miraculously, survived and was being treated in a hospital.

23 'We haven't told Nabil yet what happened,' Hayawi said. 'It will be difficult.'

24 He walked away with his son. They passed a black banner with yellow writing. It said that the Hayawi family mourned the loss of Mohammad and his nephew, 'who were assassinated by the cowardly bombing at Mutanabi Street'.

25 At 9:23 a.m. the man searching for his son spoke again.

26 'You'll find him,' he said to his relatives. 'You will find his ID, his jacket. You'll find them just as you found this,' he added, picking up the flattened shoe.

27 The men nodded and kept digging.

28 When asked how he knew his son was buried there, he replied: 'My heart tells me so.'

29 He wouldn't give his name. When asked his son's name, he answered: 'His name is Iraq.'

30 A few minutes later, he broke into tears again.

31 Iraqis passed him, gingerly stepping through the debris. Across the street from the Hayawis' bookshop, the remains of the Shahbandar Cafe sat silent. For decades, Iraqis had gathered there, waxing [speaking in a highly emotional manner] about politics and culture over water pipes and sweet tea. Beautiful black-and-white photos of Baghdad had adorned its walls.

32 At 9:48 a.m. Khalid Hussein was rattling off the names of the dead.

33 'I am trying to rebuild myself,' he said. 'We cannot leave Mutanabi Street. Outside of Mutanabi Street, we feel lost.'

34 At 10:04 a.m., a man in a green shirt stood before a shattered shop, screaming for a man named Moean.

35 'Moean. Answer me back. Moean.'

36 He fell to the ground, crying. A friend helped him up, and slowly they walked up the street, away from the debris where the five men kept digging.

In this article, the headline introduces the story, providing a sort of summary of the reported event. Paragraph 1 describes the place where the event took place and introduces the man whose drama is reported in the story. There is an attention to minute details, which involve the reader's senses (*crisp, white pages*), and particularly the sense of vision, with words related to light and colours (*pink*, *white*, *glowed*, *black*, *brown*, *dark*). The scene, described in paragraphs 1–3., is presented through the eyes of an undefined person and conveys, through carefully chosen words, the sense of desolation the man feels when he sees the destruction in front of him. It is only in the fourth paragraph that the reader finds out what caused the destruction in Mutanabi Street: *four days after a car bomb took the lives of at least 26 people and injured dozens more*. The story continues with vivid descriptions and is imbued with local people's memories and emotions. Much of what the story tells revolves around people's words and thoughts, reported through direct or indirect speech. This has the effect of making the people come alive to the reader, as well as to increase the dramatic potential of the story. The story is told chronologically, and the passing of time is emphasized by the indication of the hour at the beginning of some of the paragraphs (11, 20, 25, 32, 34). It closes (paragraph 36) with the image of a man crying as a friend helps him walk away from the scene, but leaving behind other men digging in desperation – undoubtedly a scene that cannot but be memorable to the reader.

As this example shows, narrative journalism blends the reporting of facts with the writing style of fiction to create powerful stories that promote reading through to the end.

5.5 Impersonal writing

Good reporting aims to be objective and emphasize facts, not interpretations. When writing their stories reporters should be invisible to their readers and refrain from expressing personal views and opinions. One of the ways to do that is by using an **impersonal style**.

This is achieved, firstly, by avoiding first- or second- person pronouns (*I, me, we, our, my, us, you, yours*) unless they are part of a source's direct quote. Using third-person pronouns (*he*, *she*, *they*, etc.) instead conveys an idea of distance and descriptiveness and is widely used in news stories.

Secondly, an impersonal style avoids the use of emotive words or expressions that may imply an evaluation or judgment. So, expressions like: *an interesting story*, *an impressive result*, *a tragic mistake*, *an avoidable sentence*, *a silly remark* are generally avoided, as they betray the reporter's opinion. Adjectives and other emotive expressions are acceptable if used in quotes, however, as then they report the source's and not the author's opinion. All the same, journalists can still develop their stories and give them an angle by selecting the source's words and presenting the events in a particular order.

The following article reports the story of a 20-year-old aspiring model who was killed in a car accident. The news drew a good deal of attention and sympathy in the audiences, also because the victim was young and gorgeous. In most UK papers, the news was released with an accompanying picture showing a close-up of the attractive victim.[5]

Crash victim 'an aspiring model'[6]

(Press Association, UK, September 17, 2012)

1 A young woman killed after an asylum seeker allegedly drove the wrong way down a motorway was a university-educated aspiring model, her family has said.

2 Rebecca Caine, 20, from Leeds, was a back seat passenger in a Chevrolet Matiz, when the vehicle was involved in a head on collision with a Renault Megane, coming the wrong way up the motorway, allegedly driven by Zimbabwean Wilfred Museka.

3 Miss Caine, known as Becky, died in the crash but the driver of the Matiz and two other passengers suffered only minor injuries. The

Chevrolet was heading east towards Leeds when the collision occurred at 3am on Sunday, near to junction 21 of the M62, near Milnrow, Greater Manchester.

4 Museka, 31 of Powell Street, Clayton, Manchester, appeared at Bury Magistrates' Court charged with causing death by dangerous driving and was remanded into custody.

5 In a tribute from Miss Caine's family, they said: 'As you can imagine our lives are shattered and our hearts are broken into pieces. She was a beautiful girl with her whole life ahead of her. She was embarking on a modelling career and would be finishing her final year of her business degree at Leeds University.

6 'Rebecca was a bright light that attracted everything to her with her infectious laugh and her beaming smile. She saw the best in everyone and was loved by hundreds of friends. The worst part is the emptiness and the total waste of a beautiful life. She was only 20 when she died.

7 'She was our little girl now she is our little angel. Something somewhere has failed us. We would also like to extend our sincere thanks to the police and other services for helping us through this difficult time.'

8 Museka is also charged with fraud by false representation in that he claimed to have held a full UK driving licence for 10 years to get reduced insurance premiums, driving without a licence and driving without insurance. District Judge Mark Hadfield remanded the defendant in custody to appear at Minshull Street Crown Court, Manchester, on October 8.

9 Sergeant Lee Westhead from the Serious Collision Investigation Unit, of Greater Manchester Police, said: 'A team of specialist officers are now investigating and we are providing support to the victim's family. My thoughts are with the victim's family at this terrible time.'

10 Anyone with information is asked to call the Serious Collision Investigation Unit on 0161 856 4741.

From its beginning (paragraph 1), the story opposes the figure of the woman, *a young … university-educated aspiring model*, to that of the person who caused the car crash, referred to as an *asylum seeker*. The story presents an account of the accident in paragraphs 1-3. Then paragraph 4 tells the reader that Museka, the person who allegedly caused the accident, was *charged with causing death by dangerous driving and was remanded into custody*. More information about him is given in paragraph 8, where the reader is told that man is also charged *with fraud by false representation* and that he will have to appear in court. By contrast, information about Ms Caine is given over three paragraphs (5–7), which emphasize, through her parents' words, her youth as well as her qualities both as a student and as a person. Finally, in paragraph 9, Sergeant Westhead expresses his support for the victim's family.

Thus, the story dwells on the positive characteristics of the victim, while at the same time providing little (and only negative) information about the man who caused the accident. This polarization, on the one side, helps to create a feeling of sympathy for the victim and her family and, on the other side, leaves no room for any possible justification of the man's actions.

5.6 Strategies for connecting paragraphs

News stories develop through a series of well-organized and logically connected sentences and paragraphs. The smooth, logical flow of sentences within a paragraph and a series of paragraphs in a text is called **coherence**. We will now look at some of the strategies used by journalists to create coherent stories.

From a syntactical point of view, English sentences can be linked through **co-ordination** or **subordination**. Sentences 1 and 2 below are, respectively, examples of co-ordinated and subordinated structures; the units linked together are clauses, and the linking conjunction is in italic:

1 I like English *but* I do not speak it.
2 I like English *even though* I do not speak it.

In 1 the two clauses have the same syntactic status, and neither is subordinated to the other. Each could stand on its own as an independent sentence, i.e. the main and only clause in a sentence. In 2 each clause has a different syntactic status, with the second being subordinated to the first. Co-ordinated clauses are linked by conjunctions such as *and*, *but*, *for*, *or*, *nor*, *yet*, *so*, *however*, *thus*; subordinated clauses by conjunctions such as *after*, *although*, *before*, *unless*, *whenever*, *in order that*. While co-ordination is a grammatical strategy to communicate that the actions or ideas in the two clauses have equal importance, subordination communicates that the action or idea in one of them is more important than the other, with the second being dependent on, or subordinate to, the other. Co-ordination also makes sentences easy to follow, whereas subordination increases their grammatical complexity. In news reporting, co-ordinated structures are preferred to subordinate structures because they are less complex and therefore make reading easier. When used to link paragraphs, co-ordinating conjunctions maintain paragraphs as independent units, which prevents the disruption of the text if it has to be cut for editorial reasons.

Another way to achieve paragraph coherence is by repeating **parallel structural patterns**. In the example below, the coherence of the text is created by repetition of the same Subject + Predicate structure (see also Chapter 7).

1 Sergeant Marcus Smith directed the operations ...
2 Smith ordered the following analyses ...
3 Smith added that ...

Paragraphs can also be linked by means of the **repetition of words**, including synonyms and conceptual equivalents. The use of pronouns is limited to cases where the grammatical reference to previously mentioned persons is clear and unambiguous. Finally, **hooks** are also used: words or phrases that are repeated throughout an article to give the reader a sense of unity. For example, in a story about the city council, the word 'council' used throughout the story would be a hook.

The story below exemplifies how the paragraphs in a news story are logically connected to form a coherent unit. The connection is effected by the repetition of a few lexical items, or items semantically related to them: *pet food/meat*; *meal/food*; *nutritionists/agencies/lab tests/analyses*; *makers of pet food/manufacturers*; *dog owners*.

Health food? Try the dog's dinner[7]
Pet meat has less fat than Big Mac
(Marc Horne, *The Sunday Times*, March 26, 2006)

1 THE epitaph for a horrible meal used to be 'I wouldn't feed it to my dog'. A new analysis has shown, however, that pet food is now healthier than many fast foods, containing less fat, salt and sugar.
2 Laboratory tests carried out last week found that a can of Gourmet Gold, a popular brand of cat meat, contained 2.9g of fat per 100g, one eighth the level of KFC chicken pieces and less than a third that of a McDonald's Big Mac or a Pizza Hut pizza.
3 Cesar dog food contained 4.4g of fat per 100g, higher than the cat meat but still much lower than fast foods. Levels of salt and sugar in the pet food were also substantially lower than in the human meals.
4 Nutritionists said this weekend that the findings highlighted the continuing problem of unhealthy amounts of fat, salt and sugar in food.
5 Earlier this month the Food Standards Agency launched a red, amber and green 'traffic light' scheme to indicate on food packaging the proportion of unhealthy ingredients.
6 'On all levels the cat and dog foods that we analysed would be categorized in the green or amber levels, while some convenience foods aimed at humans would fall in the red or unhealthy category,' said John Searle, the scientist who carried out the pet food analysis at the government-accredited Global food-testing laboratory in Burton-upon-Trent.
7 'It would not do a human any harm to eat this cat and dog food. The taste would be a bit different from what you'd expect, but nutritionally it is fine.'

8 Makers of pet food include the same multinationals – such as Nestlé and Mars – that make commonly eaten snacks.

9 Manufacturers point out that pet food is designed for a different purpose from human food. Pet owners must be able to use the same food to give the animal all its nutritional requirements day after day. Humans, by contrast, expect variety and can balance out unhealthy meals with healthy ones.

10 Manufacturers say fast foods should be seen as an occasional treat rather than an everyday meal. However, Jeanette Longfield, co-ordinator of Sustain, which campaigns for better food and farming, said: 'I hope this acts as a wake-up call for manufacturers and shoppers.'

11 Dog owners said this weekend they were unsurprised by the findings, adding that over the past decade there had been substantial advances in knowledge about animal nutrition and the composition of pet food.

12 Jim Barnes, vice-chairman of Bearsden dog training club in Glasgow, who owns two cocker spaniels, said: 'It has got to be nutritious. If the dog is not getting proper nutrition it can affect growth and even mood by turning animals aggressive or hyperactive.'

13 Pet food has been heavily regulated in recent decades. All ingredients must, according to European Union law, be fit for human consumption.

14 The meat has usually been rejected for humans as it is mangled or discoloured or comes from parts of the animal, such as lungs, rarely eaten in Britain.

15 Pet food cannot, however, include material such as spinal cord, which was excluded from the human food chain following the BSE crisis.

16 Manufacturers in the £1.5 billion-a-year market are even introducing 'gourmet' touches with recipes that include pasta, steamed vegetables, risotto and Mediterranean herbs.

17 To investigate whether the wholesomeness of pet food still comes at the expense of flavour, *The Sunday Times* carried out a taste test last week. Anna Lawlor, 25, from Streatham, south London, gave her verdict on premium pet foods and items bought in supermarkets.

18 The items she compared included a Ginster's Cornish Pastie and a spoonful of a leading dog meat – Butcher's chicken, ham and pea casserole.

19 'When I tried the meaty dog food and the pastie, I could identify the pastie because it was so heavily seasoned, whereas the dog food tasted more meaty,' said Lawlor.

20 For comparison, Rye, her parents' eight-year-old mongrel, was given a Big Mac. He wolfed it down.

21 The laboratory analysis found some positive signs for human food – fibre, for example, which is an important aid to digestion, was lower in the pet food.

22 However, on key measures the pet food came out well. The unhealthiest fast food item was KFC chicken pieces, which contain 23.2g of fat per 100g and 1.9g of salt. If a KFC meal is eaten with fries, the figures are lower. While a McDonald's Big Mac contains 10.7g of fat per 100g, a combined meal with fries has an average 12g.

23 In addition to the products tested in the laboratory, 30 human foods and 15 pet foods were compared using their labels. The pet food consistently outperformed the human in terms of health.

24 All food manufacturers insisted this weekend they were taking steps to offer healthier options and cut salt levels. A spokesman for Unilever said there was a limit to the changes that could be introduced to make food healthier. 'It cannot be so extreme that we drive people away,' he said.

25 'We eat to enjoy. Taste and texture elements are very important to how we enjoy food.'

Students' activities

Activity 1

Look at a newspaper either in print or online. Are there stories written in the Inverted Pyramid style? In the Hourglass style? In the narrative style? What kinds of stories (hard news or soft news) tend to be written in each style?

Activity 2

Look at the story in section 5.3.1. Analyse how paragraphs are connected in the story. Mark with a highlighting pen all the conjunctions, parallel structural patterns and repeated words or concepts that are used to connect the paragraphs.

Activity 3

Repeat activity 2 with the story in section 5.4.1. How do the two structures compare as regards strategies for connecting paragraphs?

Activity 4

An exercise rewriting the story 'Anguish in the Ruins of Mutanabi Street'.

For this activity you can try rewriting the story in section 5.4.1 using the Inverted Pyramid style. Before you start writing:

- Analyse the story;
- Identify the part of the story that you would use in the lead and order the elements in the story in decreasing order of importance;

- Decide which quotes would be relevant to keep and which could be paraphrased or summarized;
- You may first want to go online and search for comparable stories written on the same topic, by entering some key words like: *Baghdad book market bombed*. This step is optional.

You can then start writing the story. When writing it, you should avoid using language that in the original text is meant to create an emotional impact on the reader (e.g., *anguish*, *mourning loved ones*, *once-unifying place*), or that involves the readers' senses (such as colours, sounds, etc.). Remember that the ending should contain events that are not memorable or particularly relevant.

Further reading

Conley, D., and Lamble, S. 2006. *The Daily Miracle: An Introduction to Journalism*, Oxford, Oxford University Press.

Cotter, C. 2010. *News Talk: Investigating the Language of Journalism*, Cambridge, Cambridge University Press.

Grunwald E., and Lauridsen, J. 2007. 'Distribution and use of image-evoking language constructions in written news', *Nordicom Review*, 28, 2, 93–109.

Hartsock, J.C. 2000. *A History of American Literary Journalism: The Emergence of a Modern Narrative Form*, Amherst, University of Massachusetts Press.

Herbert, J. 2000. *Journalism in the Digital Age*, Oxford, Focal Press.

Missouri Group (B.S. Brooks, G. Kennedy, D.R. Moen and D. Ranly). 2005. *News Reporting and Writing*, 5th ed., New York, Bedford/St Martin's.

Nel, F. 2005. *Writing for the Media in Southern Africa*, 3rd ed., Cape Town, Oxford University Press.

Pavlik, J.V. 2001. *Journalism and New Media,* New York, Columbia University Press.

Scanlan, C. 2002. *Reporting and Writing Basics for the 21st Century*, New York, Oxford University Press.

Wilkinson, J.S., Grant, A.E., and Fisher, D.J. 2009. *Principles of Convergent Journalism*, New York and Oxford, Oxford University Press.

Chapter 6

Headline, lead and story proper

This chapter examines the linguistic features characteristic of news story headlines, leads and the body copy. The focus is on headlines – their grammatical characteristics, and the rhetorical strategies used to create them in print and online news, with many examples provided – but the main characteristics of leads and body copy are also examined.

6.1 The components of a news story

News story texts are typically structured into four parts that serve different purposes (see Figure 4.2). At the top of the story is the **headline**, which is meant to attract the attention of the reader and announce what the story is about. A **byline** follows, showing the name of the reporter and the date of the report. The story then consists of an introduction, or **lead** (the first paragraph in the story), which provides a synopsis of the story by outlining the most important facts, and finally the news story proper, or **body copy**, which contains all the information and details.

6.2 The headline

The headline has the important function of **grabbing the readers' attention** and giving them an idea of the news story's content and tone, so that they can decide whether it is worth reading or not. The headline is generally one line (much less frequently, two lines) long, printed in large type and written in a telegraphic style. Headlines are generally not written by the reporter, but by the sub-editor, who decides on the page layout and chooses the wording and the type font and size that can best fit the design of the page. Thus, they are often written *after* the story, and are extracted from its lead or based on its main points. They must sound interesting and appealing, while respecting strict space constraints. Because headlines need to be concise, informative and at the same time attractive, headline writing is considered one of the most creative aspects of journalism.

6.2.1 *Grammar of headlines*

In headlines, the need to use condensed, highly **synthetic language** has led to the development of a specific syntax, which preserves lexical words (words that carry the main meaning units, such as nouns, adjectives, adverbs, main verbs), but omits function words: those that serve a grammatical function, such as determiners (i.e., *the, a, an, this that*) or auxiliary verbs (i.e., forms of the verbs *be, have, do*). The headlines below illustrate this.

No criminal charges in wrong-way crash
(the *New York Times*, August 18, 2009)

California to get $1.5-billion loan from JPMorgan Chase
(*Los Angeles Times*, August 18, 2009)

At least 95 dead as series of blasts shakes Baghdad
(the *Guardian*, August 19, 2009)

China to invest in TV digitalization in Africa
(chinadaily.com.cn, August 27, 2012)

Beheaded her son, but 'no threat'
(*New Zealand Herald*, August 19, 2009)

Eyes on Isaac...
(boston.cbslocal.com, August 28, 2012)

9 things never to tell your hubby
(*The Times of India*, August 27, 2012)

Ancient fortress believed to have been used to annex Dokdo found
(*The Korea Times*, August 28, 2012)

Another grammatical feature exploited in headlines is the use of **nominalizations** (nouns derived from verbs or adjectives, often, but not always, with a change in the word ending). A few examples are shown below. In the last three there is no change in the word ending.

departure	from	*depart*	*difficulty*	from	*difficult*
arrival	from	*arrive*	*difference*	from	*different*
expansion	from	*expand*	*depth*	from	*deep*
exclusion	from	*exclude*	*sensitivity*	from	*sensitive*
eating	from	*eat*	*redness*	from	*red*
hope	from	*hope*			
answer	from	*answer*			
say	from	*say*			

Nominalization has the effect of presenting events and properties as if they were things or concepts. By making the action or quality reported more abstract, nominalizations provide journalists with a powerful tool to increase the perceived level of objectivity and formal distance of their news. Stylistically, nominalized forms can be used as nouns which can be placed in different positions in the sentence (for example, they can be preceded by adjectives or prepositions, or they can be used as subjects or direct objects), and thus give the journalist a high degree of flexibility in creating the headline.[1] This is illustrated in the examples below (nominalizations are underlined).

> **Zoo welcomes arrival of baby tapir**
>
> (the *Guardian*, February 12, 2012)

> **Failure to communicate: Does text instead of talk create a communication divide?**
>
> (the *Oakland Press*, June 17, 2012)

> **Australian in match-fixing revelation**
>
> (www.thetimes.co.uk, August 19, 2009)

> **Denying the war on women**
>
> (www.NBCNews.com, August 28, 2012)

> **Measuring up**
>
> (*San Jose Mercury News*, August 28, 2012)

> **Kids crossing the cultural divide**
>
> (chinadaily.com.cn, August 28, 2012)

In many newspapers or online news sites, a secondary headline is also found, called a **deck head, summary line** or **summary blurb**, which, together with the headline, provides a short summary of the main story facts. The following is an example of a headline with a summary line:

> **Girl who went missing 18 years ago found in California**
> Authorities say Jaycee Lee Dugard walked into a police station and identified herself
>
> (the *Guardian*, August 27, 2009)

6.2.2 'Witty' headlines

A news story is always competing for the reader's attention with advertising and other news on the same page and in the paper. To create 'attractive' headlines and catch the reader's attention, a number of linguistic, rhetorical or stylistic devices may be used.

One of these is to create 'witty' headlines, i.e., those that entice readers by engaging them in some intellectual game. Witty headlines are particularly common in British newspapers, and more so in tabloids; however, this strategy is not confined to the UK. As explained in section 6.2.3 below, witty headlines occur more frequently in print than in online news.

One way in which headlines can attract the reader is by creating a wordplay that makes reference to other texts of various kinds (idiomatic expressions, well-known sayings, literary quotations, poems, book or movie titles, names of famous people, movies, dramas, etc.). This is a form of what in linguistics is called **intertextuality**. Here are some headlines containing intertextual references, with explanations.

> **To wash or not to wash**
> Pesticide row over advice on fruit and vegetables
> (*Daily Express*, March 27, 2002)

Here Hamlet's well-known dilemma 'To be or not to be' has been reworded (replacing the verb 'be' with the verb *wash*) to introduce a story on the controversy over the use of pesticides in fruit and vegetables.

> **Sue's that girl**
> Meet new member of UK's top gossip team
> (the *Daily Mirror*, April 15, 2002)

The headline introduces the story of a person named Sue and alludes to one of the popular singer Madonna's most famous early songs 'Who's That Girl', replacing 'Who's' for *Sue's*.

> **Potholes bite the dust**
> (*International Express*, February 5, 2002)

The idiomatic expression 'bite the dust', meaning 'fall to the ground, wounded or dead',[2] is used to introduce a story about the possible solution of the problem of potholes blighting Britain's roads. The expression is used in a quasi-literal meaning, with potholes figuratively depicted as biting (i.e., eating) the dust of the streets.

> **From Russia with Gloves**
> (*Los Angeles Sentinel*, July 16, 2009)

Here, the headline introducing a story about a Russian welterweight champion alludes to the 1963 James Bond movie 'From Russia with Love', replacing 'love' with *gloves*. This headline seems to have been circulating for a number of years in different contexts, showing how headlines may be reusable, repeat clichés, or create conventions.[3]

Word association is another favoured writing technique. The following example, from a story discussing Afghani refugees coming to a UN camp on the outskirts of Kabul, reminds the reader of the common expression 'home, sweet home'. Note that, by creating a contrast between the word 'barren' and the implied word *sweet*, the headline aims to hint at the situation of the refugees living in an inhospitable environment, thus setting the tone of the story.

Home, barren, home

(abcnews.go.com, May 7, 2009)

Headlines can also contain allusions to well-known facts or people, as in the example provided below.

Thank Gord he 'saved world'

(www.thesun.co.uk, December 10, 2008)

This headline introduces a story based on the words used by former British Prime Minister Gordon Brown, when he accidentally declared that he had saved the world from economic ruin. The article picks up on the Prime Minister's words by comparing him to God: the name 'Gordon' is abbreviated to *Gord* and an allusion is made to biblical events – like God, Gord 'saved the world'.

The attractiveness of headlines may often depend on the **play with spellings and sounds**. This may be done using rhetorical devices, such as rhymes, alliterations, onomatopoeia, etc. The following headlines show a play with sounds.

The rape the tape

(the *Daily Mirror*, November 12, 2002)

In this headline, the rhyming words *rape* and *tape* are used to introduce the story of a tape in possession of one of the British Royal family's butlers (Paul Burrell), containing details of the alleged rape of a royal household staff member.

The following headline shows an example of alliteration: all the main words begin with the same vowel. This is done to highlight the main concept on which the story focuses: animals in cold Alaska.

Animalistic antics in arctic Alaska
Jennifer Sharples shares her experience of life in the wilderness

(the *Weekly Telegraph*, February 12, 2002)

In the next example, the headline engages the reader in a word play involving the sound made by cats (*purr*) and the homophony between the syllables *purr* and *per* (as in *per-fect*). It seems a good way to attract attention to a story about cats.

> **Purr-fect opportunity**
>
> (*New York Post*, April 4, 2002)

In a similar fashion, in the next example, the headline plays with the similarity between the initial sounds in the word *bird*, pronounced /bər/, and the exclamation one makes when shivering with cold, commonly written as *brrr* and pronounced /bər/. The play on the two word sounds is used to introduce a story about red-winged blackbirds freezing in a record-breaking chill in Woolwich, Maine.

> **Brrrrrrrrr-die**
>
> (*San Francisco Chronicle*, April 19, 2003)

The content of the story is also played upon in the second part of the headline, a homograph of the verb *die*.

The use of this strategy has become quite conventional. There are many examples of headlines containing a play on the sounds /pər/ or /bər/ used for stories about cats and cold respectively. 'Bullied chicken finds the purrfect pals' (*Manchester Evening News*, August 21, 2009) heads a story about a chicken making friends with a group of cats; 'Brrrr-aving Alaska' (*San Petersburg Times* online, February 23, 2003) advertises travel to Alaska; and 'Polar Brrrr Gals' (*New York Post*, January 2, 2008) introduces a story on couples participating in the annual Polar Bears Club charity swim on New Year's Day.

Finally, headlines can engage the reader by including a **pun.** Puns exploit word ambiguity to humorous or rhetorical effect. Such ambiguity can arise through:

- word polysemy (the multiple meanings of words). For example, the word *book* can mean both 'a volume' and 'make a reservation';
- words that carry connotative associations: that is, words that have an emotional meaning associated with them, which can be positive or negative. For example, both *childish* and *youthful* can be used to describe people, but while the former implies that someone is immature, the latter suggests someone lively and energetic.
- words having similar or identical sounds but different meanings (homophones): for example, *herd* and *heard*; *flour* and *flower*; *to*, *two*, and *too*.

In the following example, a pun is created by replacing one letter in the original word *Baghdad* with two letters in the second syllable of the word, yielding the nonsense word *Baghdead*, which reminds the readers of the phrase *dead in Baghdad*. This headline was in fact used to call attention to the death of Saddam Hussein in Baghdad in 2006.

> **Baghdead**
>
> (*The Sunday Times*, December 30, 2006).

Headlines may also contain expressions taken from everyday life, but which acquire a different meaning in the context of the story the newspaper tells, and so succeed in grabbing the reader's attention. For example, the headline below is about artist Damien Hirst's exhibit, featuring flayed cows' heads to represent Christ's Apostles. The colloquial exclamation *Holy cow!* is here intentionally used both as an exclamation and to refer to the artist's exploration of the religious significance of cows' heads.

> **Holy cow! Hirst turns to religion**
>
> (the *Daily Telegraph*, September 9, 2003).

Metaphors, too, are exploited in headlines to engage the reader by setting up analogies between otherwise distinct concepts. In financial news, a particularly fruitful metaphor is that of fish in the sea. The image of sharks in the first example below is one often found in economic/financial news stories and is generally used to describe speculators or unscrupulous investors. Connected to this is the idea of swimming in dangerous waters, seen in the second example. The third headline presents an image of investors fishing for stocks.

> **Swimming with sharks as scandals mount**
>
> (www.marketwatch.com, July 18, 2012)

> **Investors dip into riskier waters**
>
> (online.wsj.com, April 1, 2012)

> **Nikkei inches up as investors fish for oversold stocks**
>
> (www.reuters.com, August 14, 2012)

6.2.3 Informative headlines

Headlines can also be written in a way that privileges the informative, descriptive element, by appealing to reason rather than emotions. Informative headlines are favoured in authoritative papers and are suitable for tragic stories, where wit or double meanings that create puns or humorous effects would be considered inappropriate. More importantly, informative headlines are favoured in online news, because they tend to be descriptive and contain keywords. This makes them more retrievable by online search engines than witty headlines, and so they can appear high in search rankings. At the same time, because reading patterns on the web differ from reading patterns on paper, informative headlines appear more suitable to the needs of online users who scan pages and rapidly decide whether headline links are worth clicking on or not.

In general, informative headlines are characterized by simple, straight direct sentences and active verbs in the present tense. Here are some examples.

> **Survey documents popularity of alternative treatments**
> (*Washington Post*, December 10, 2008)

> **Flat price frustrates farmers**
> (the *Independent*, Bangladesh, August 26, 2012)

> **Cycling may go into a decline**
> (*DNA Sunday*, India, August 26, 2012)

> **Wen reduces fiscal burden for exporters**
> (*Global Times*, China, August 27, 2012)

Informative headlines may also provide information on the **tone** of the article. In the example that follows the headline introduces a story about young men's obsession with exercise, possibly promoted by men's magazines.

> **Lads' mags inflict preening curse**
> Readers obsess over exercise.
>
> The laddish culture promoted by men's magazines has spawned a new medical condition: athletica nervosa, or an obsession with exercise.
> (*The Sunday Times*, March 16, 2008)

This headline is both ironic and witty. It provides an interpretative key to the tone of the news story, which one may expect will be ironic too. The sense of irony in the headline stems from the contrast between the colloquial words (*Lads' mags*) chosen to introduce the topic (men's magazines) and the rather formal expression *inflict curse*. The choice of the word *preening* to describe men's care of their bodies is also ironical. Finally, the expression *inflict preening curse* is uncommon and rather anomalous, and certainly not obvious. The lead explains the expression, specifying that it refers to a newly discovered condition affecting men reading men's magazines that promote an obsession with exercise.

6.3 The lead

When readers are attracted to an article, after reading the headline and looking at the picture and the picture caption, the next thing they are going to read is the lead. Leads are news story introductions, as well their first and most important paragraphs. Their function is to give readers an immediate sense of what the article is about and make them want to read more. Typically, leads are one paragraph long, consist of a single sentence, and do not exceed 25 words. In the case of stories that cannot be summarized in so few words, a second sentence can be used, but the idea is that succinct leads create a more powerful impact and are easier to read.

There are two main types of lead: Direct (or summary) leads and Delayed leads. **Direct leads** are used for conventional hard news stories, and, in general, for any story that uses the Inverted Pyramid style. Direct leads reveal immediately what the story is about by providing a summary, at a minimum, of the most newsworthy *who*, *what*, *where* and *when* of the story. Linguistically, direct leads appear to expand on the information contained in the headline (though in fact the headline is likely to be drawn from the lead and not *vice versa*). The language is simple, sentences are often structured with simple subject–predicate–object syntax and characterized by concise and clear language to keep the message brief and immediate.

Here are two examples of direct leads:

> **Pets offered to help Internet addicts**
> The government is providing animal companions to help Internet addicts recover from their addiction.
> (*The Korea Times*, August 29, 2012)

> **Primary school maths failures on the rise**
> The number of seven-year-olds failing to master basic maths skills increased this year despite government efforts to drive up standards.
> (www.thetimes.co.uk, August 26, 2009)

Both leads consist of one sentence that summarizes the main contents of the article. In the second lead, the information is presented in a highly condensed form, and the grammatical subject of the sentence is a long nominal group (*The number of seven-year-olds failing to master basic maths skills*); this first long nominal group is followed by another long and nominal group (*government efforts to drive up standards*). The presence of long nominal groups, which result from the journalist's need to compress concepts into a few words, may in fact hamper the intelligibility of the lead.

Like direct leads, **delayed leads** must capture the essence of the story and make the reader want to continue. But, unlike direct leads, they can be a few paragraphs long, and, more importantly, they temporarily withhold the relation of the facts. That is, they introduce the story through an anecdote, a significant detail, an emblem, which sets the scene or evokes a mood. The aim is to create a sense of suspense or anticipated surprise. For this reason, delayed leads are most often used on softer news stories that are peculiar, bizarre, amusing or moving. After the delayed lead, the story continues with the so-called **nut paragraph(s)**, providing more information in decreasing order of importance as in the Inverted Pyramid.

An example of a delayed lead can be found in the story below, which describes how wives' can perfect their high-tech skills to spy on their husbands.

Suspicious wives master the art of high-tech spying[4]
(Andy Dolan, www.dailymail.co.uk, May 24, 2010)

1 Men have long maintained that they're better at mastering technology than women are.

2 However, there's one field where they appear to have fallen far behind.

3 Research shows that suspicious wives are almost twice as likely as their husbands to spy on their spouse's online activities.

4 This suggests that, when it comes to snooping on their partner, they are quicker to embrace the power of computers and mobile phones.

5 According to the survey of almost 1,000 married middle-aged couples, 14 per cent of the wives secretly read their husbands' emails, while 13 per cent admitted poring over their beloved's text messages.

6 Of the husbands questioned, only eight per cent admitted reading their wives' emails, while seven per cent had checked text messages sent to their partner.

7 Researchers from the London School of Economics and Nottingham Trent University asked the couples questions about internet use to investigate what role the web and text messaging plays in maintaining intimate 'offline' relationships – and whether its use was a cause of conflict between partners.

8 The study appears to show that some women may develop their IT skills simply to improve their surveillance techniques.

9 Dr Ellen Helsper, a lecturer in the media and communications department of the LSE, who led the study, said: 'Our findings showed that there are surprisingly high levels of surveillance.

10 'One of the surprising findings was that surveillance was undertaken more often by wives than husbands. This contrasts with research that suggests that women are less technologically skilled than men.

11 'It seems that they are able to overcome these barriers when they feel their relationship is at stake.'

12 The study, entitled 'Netiquette within married couples', analysed data from 940 couples with an average age of 49 who had been married for an average of 19 years.
13 It found ten per cent of couples admitted that each had secretly read their partner's emails. Ten per cent of couples admitted to reading their spouse's text messages when his or her back was turned.
14 Ten per cent of women and six per cent of men had also checked the browser history of their partners. In a further four per cent of relationships, both said they had.
15 The findings were reported in the American journal *Computers in Human Behavior* in March.

In this story, the first two paragraphs have the function of leading up to the third paragraph, which is the real lead of the story, and presents a condensed summary of it. Following the structure of the Inverted Pyramid, the paragraph following the lead expands on it, and the following paragraphs provide information in decreasing order of importance, as explained in the following section. Paragraphs 9–15, occurring after a page break in the original text, provide the scientific information behind the report. Because this information is found at the end of the story, it is clearly not meant to be in focus.

6.4 The paragraphs after the lead

After the lead, the story builds upon the points made in the lead. The first few paragraphs after the lead, and particularly the first five, need to keep the reader engaged in the story. Thus, they need to present the facts, and include any detail that needs explanation or questions that the reader might have.

Typically, the second and third paragraphs expand upon the lead. The information presented is aimed at telling the reader *why* the reported event is significant. If the event is about a famous person, the significance may be because of *who* they are; at this point a more in-depth paragraph may provide background information to explain why the person is important in relation to the reported event.

After the lead has been supported by expanding and clarifying the main points of the story, succeeding paragraphs can go into further detail about the event by including, for example, a biographical sketch of the person the story is about, historical or socio-cultural information, or any other background information that may add interest and contextualize the story.

Finally, the story ends with a set of paragraphs that add information that is non-crucial to the story and that can be easily cut from the bottom up, leaving the remaining paragraphs to stand as a coherent and cohesive report.

6.4.1 Structuring information in a news story: an example

The article below offers an example of how information in news stories is structured as a series of paragraphs that provide support to the lead, add background information and, finally, offer a conclusion with little informative content.

A short, 30-word lead introduces the main character of the story, Oliver Jufer; it places him where the event occurred, Thailand, and it anticipates the consequences of his actions: he is getting himself in trouble for drinking too much and committing an act of vandalism.

Paragraph 2 expands on the lead and amplifies what was adumbrated there, namely that the 'bother' Jufer got himself into is a possible jail sentence of 75 years, and that the reason for it is that he damaged posters of the King. Paragraph 3 expands on this and explains why Mr Jufer's action is considered so serious in Thailand. Paragraphs 4 and 5 give the reader the background and chronological details of the story, which have been delayed until after the story introduction, following the practice used in the Inverted Pyramid style. All the details presented after paragraph 5 are less crucial to the development of the story, and could be omitted without much loss of information.

Moment of vandalism may lead to a lifetime in prison[5]

(Richard Lloyd Parry, *The Times,* March 13, 2007)

1 Oliver Jufer is not the first foreigner in Thailand to make a nuisance of himself after too many drinks, but few small-time vandals have found themselves in as much bother.

2 Mr Jufer, a 57-year-old Swiss, faces a jail sentence of 75 years, not because of the damage he caused but because of what he damaged: posters of the country's monarch, King Bhumibol Adulyadej.

3 He pleaded guilty yesterday in the city of Chiang Mai to five counts of *lèse-majesté* – the crime of insulting the monarchy. Mr Jufer's prosecution draws attention to one of the most curious anomalies about Thailand: a country shockingly tolerant in some respects, but intolerant even of the slightest criticism of its Royal Family.

4 The crime was committed last December on the 79th birthday of King Bhumibol, the world's longest-reigning monarch, who celebrated 60 years on the throne last summer. To honour the occasion, sales of alcohol were stopped early, and this appears to have triggered Mr Jufer's frustration.

5 He was caught on surveillance cameras spraying black paint over a few of the millions of portraits of the King seen in towns and cities. After his arrest, he denied the crimes of insulting the King and defacing public property, but pleaded guilty yesterday to the five charges, each carrying a minimum sentence of three years and a maximum of fifteen.

6 The hearing was held behind closed doors, and Mr Jufer said nothing to journalists as he entered and left the court in orange prison overalls with his legs shackled. 'Revealing the details of this case does not benefit anybody because it involves the King and the monarchy,' the prosecutor, Bhanu Kwanyuen, said. 'In every Thai Constitution the King is revered and worshipped, and he cannot be insulted. Thai people cannot accept this.'

7 Despite the *lèse-majesté* laws having been on the statute books since 1959, the authorities appear exceedingly embarrassed about using them to prosecute, perhaps conscious of how anachronistic and draconian they appear. The laws have never been invoked by members of the Royal Family. Instead, individual citizens are empowered to bring charges against others. In the past few years they have been used mainly by rival politicians to accuse one another of disloyalty to the monarchy.

8 Ironically the only person with the nerve to question the *lèse-majesté* laws has been King Bhumibol. 'When you say the King can do no wrong, it is wrong,' he said on his 78th birthday, a year to the day before Mr Jufer's tantrum. 'Actually I must also be criticized. Because if you say the King cannot be criticized, it means that the King is not human.'

Students' activities

Activity 1

Study the headlines of a tabloid. Count how many witty and informative headlines there are. Do the same same with a broadsheet or Berliner. Choose a few witty headlines from any of the papers and try to rewrite them to make them informative headlines.

Activity 2

Look at the headlines below. Which headline makes use of the rhetorical and linguistic strategies shown in the box?

alliteration, pun, rhyme, intertextual reference, nominalization, synthetic language (specify which words are omitted).

Batty butty ban	(the *Sun*, UK, April 29, 2010)
No predicting the future	(*The Times of India*, India, November 17, 2012)
Sleepy bus driver guilty in fatal crash	(*Queens Chronicle*, USA, November 15, 2012)
Lights go up	(the *Anniston Star*, USA, November 16, 2012)
Fear Factor	(the *Sun*, Malaysia, November 16, 2012)
FREED!	(*Daily Observer*, Jamaica, November 16, 2012)
Goldbye!	(the *Daily Mirror*, UK, August 13, 2012)
Trivial pursuit	(the *Courier Mail*, Australia, November 16, 2012)
Green Tape, Red Tape	(*Hobart Mercury*, Australia, February 2, 2013)

Activity 3

All the headlines in the list below make use of synthetic language. Rewrite them by adding any word that has been omitted.

Plan's lack of light rail 'short sighted'
(the *Press*, Australia, November 16, 2012)

Reforms outlined
(*Las Vegas Review Journal*, US, November 16, 2012)

Massive freeway overhaul on way
(the *Dallas Morning News*, US, November 16, 2012)

Blackberry 10 to be launched in January, RIM announces
(www.bbc.co.uk, November 11, 2012)

Duo pretended to be mother and daughter
(www.nzherald.co.nz, November l6, 2012)

Activity 4

Creating headlines from leads.

Create appropriate headlines for the leads in the list below. Use features like verb and determiner deletion, nominalizations, complex noun groups, etc.

Example:

> LOS ANGELES – 'Despicable Me' continues to wow family audiences in 23 international territories, earning an impressive $19.1 million this past weekend, well on its way to a $500 million worldwide gross.
> (www.gmanetwork.com, November 4, 2010)

'Despicable' on way to $500 million worldwide

1 A two-year-old boy was banned from eating cheese sandwiches at a council-run nursery unless his parents added a lettuce leaf.

(www.telegraph.co.uk, April 28, 2010)

2 Even though he wore a wig and sunglasses, a bank robber's lip piercing helped a Wyomissing Hills bank teller recognize him, police said Wednesday.

(readingeagle.com, October 22, 2009)

3 Greece halted foreign mail deliveries Wednesday after nearly a dozen small parcel bombs were discovered addressed to the leaders of France, Germany and Italy and foreign embassies in Athens.

(www.france24.com, November 3, 2010)

4 Melvis Kwok is the city's best-known impersonator of the rock 'n' roll legend known here as the Cat King. Decades after Elvis Presley's death, he is still revered around Asia.

(www.nytimes.com, November 4, 2010)

5 A Zimbabwean has been killed by a pride of lions while he was showering in a camp in the country's north.

(www.telegraph.co.uk, November 3, 2010)

6 A 9-month-old baby is in critical condition at an Atlanta hospital after she was attacked by two raccoons while sleeping in her crib in the same room as her mother.

(Associated Press, November 3, 2010)

7 Universities in England will be able to charge tuition fees of up to £9,000 per year, as the government transfers much of the cost of courses to students.

(www.bbc.co.uk, November 3, 2010)

Further reading

Conley, D., and Lamble, S. 2006. *The Daily Miracle: An Introduction to Journalism*, Oxford, Oxford University Press.

Durant, A., and Lambrou, M. 2009. *Language and Media: A Resource Book for Students*, London and New York, Routledge.

Lohr, S. 2006. 'This boring headline is written for Google', www.nytimes.com, April 9, 2006.

McKane, A. 2006. *Newswriting*, London, Sage.

Nel, F. 2005. *Writing for the Media in Southern Africa*, 3rd ed., Cape Town, Oxford University Press.

Reah, D. 2002. *The Language of Newspapers*, London and New York, Routledge.
Rich, C. 2003. *Writing and Reporting News*, Boston MA, Wadsworth/Thomson Learning.
Spool, J. 2006. 'Boring headlines or great links?', www.uie.com/brainsparks/2006/04/11/boring-headlines-or-great-links.

Chapter 7

The tools of the trade

This chapter examines the linguistic strategies journalists can use to compact lots of information in a short text. It also explains and exemplifies how the choice of verbs, sentence structure, and active or passive voice allow the journalist to highlight information and convey a point of view.

7.1 The 'kiss and tell' principle

At the basis of news writing is the so-called 'kiss and tell' principle. This expresses the essence of good journalism: *k*eep *i*t *s*hort and *s*imple *and tell* the story. In line with this principle, news stories are written in simple and concise language, which means that short and native English words are preferred over long and Latinate ones, and there is a tendency to avoid complex sentences with subordinate clauses.

The preference for concise language in news reporting has its historical roots in the nineteenth century, when it helped to keep down the cost of transmitting long and complex texts over the telegraph. Today, the content (and often also the size) of news stories is determined by the need to increase revenues; if they contain words and structures that are sharp and to the point, news stories contribute to economies in the newspaper's production by reducing the costs associated with journalism. In online news production, the preference for brevity is motivated by the expected reception of the text by the envisaged end-user. Concise stories are more appealing to the Internet reader who is often simply skimming web pages to collect pieces of information and may be unwilling to read long articles due to lack of time. In both cases, the 'kiss and tell' principle has an essential role in news writing.

7.2 Well-packaged information

The need for concision in news reporting has contributed to a style that packs as much information as possible into a text that is as short as possible. This style is characterized by a preference for nominal structures over verbal structures (nouns rather than verbs). As part of this process, nominalizations and long, complex noun groups are frequently used.

In Chapter 6, we introduced the concept of **nominalization**, a process that enables actions or events to be described as entities (i.e., things or concepts) by transforming verbs (and adjectives) into nouns. As part of this transformation, the *process* being reported may end up being deleted, and, as a result, the action or event loses contextualization and becomes more abstract. Compare the expressions below, where each pair conveys the same content, but formulated differently. (Nominalizations are underlined):

	Non-nominalized form	Nominalized form
1	We donated to charity. This made us happy.	Our charity donation made us happy.
2	The problem is complex and needs to be solved.	The complexity of the problem needs a solution.
3	He writes wonderfully. I like it.	I like his wonderful writing.
4	Students must apply to college now.	Students' college applications are due now.
5	The Dutch Prime Minister arrived late.	The Dutch Prime Minister's late arrival.
6	There was not enough funding. This meant that the project had to be abandoned.	The lack of funding led to the abandonment of the project.

As the examples show, often the nominalized expressions use fewer words than the non-nominalized, and they convey information in a more compact form, with fewer clauses than in non-nominalized structures. However, the nominal constructions become more abstract and more complex to understand, because they do not refer to the primary participants involved in the events being reported – namely the subjects of the predicates in the non-nominalized versions. This is particularly true when they create long and complex noun groups like the ones in 4 and 5 above.

Nominalizations are a useful tool in news reporting because they allow the writer to manage and control the information flow in a sentence. As the examples above show, a verb that is nominalized can occur in a sentence wherever a noun, or noun phrase can occur: it can be made into the subject of a verb, a direct or indirect object, or the object of a preposition, and can be premodified by an adjective. Such flexibility lets the journalist move the focus of information around within the sentence, and do so for stylistic, logical or argumentative reasons. Here is an example of the flexibility that nominalizations allow (nominalizations are underlined):

Non-nominalized form	Nominalized form
The candidates heatedly debated immigration issues.	• Immigration was at the heart of the candidates' heated debate. • The candidates' immigration debate heated up. • There was a heated debate over immigration issues.

As we can see, using nominalizations creates **complex noun groups** of two or three words, and sometimes more. However, the sentence structures are rather simple, consisting of subject + predicate + object/object of preposition.

Complex noun groups are frequently used in written English. They can be characterized as strings of words that together realize a syntactic-semantic unit. The construction involves a head noun, the nucleus of the unit, optionally preceded by a determiner, adverbs, adjectives and other nouns. As the examples below show, the head is the last word in the group, and the meaning can be worked out by moving backwards from the head.

Complex noun group	Meaning
1 Proposed labour-market reforms	= reforms on the market of labour that have been proposed
2 Community-based instruction package	= package of instructions based on the community
3 Last-minute home vacation rental deals	= deals for renting a vacation home that you can find at the last minute

Complex noun groups are often used in news reporting because they create condensed structures containing a lot of information that can be packed and moved in the sentence. This typical feature of news reporting is exploited particularly for texts that are written under severe space limitations, for example portable electronic devices such as smart phones and tablets.

Below are some examples of complex noun groups in news story headlines and stories.

1 Japanese catwalk robot unveiled
(www.telegraph.co.uk, March 16, 2009)

2 China coalmine blast death toll jumps to 87
(AP, AT&T news service, November 23, 2009)

3 About 125 Harvard University undergraduates are being investigated for cheating in a final exam last year, the largest academic misconduct scandal in the prestigious institution's history.
(timesofindia.indiatimes.com, August 31, 2012)

4 Missing Colorado girl Jessica Ridgeway's body believed found
(abcnews.go.com, October 11, 2012).

7.2.1 An example from a news story

The article below, dealing with baggage problems at London Heathrow airport, shows nominal structures used in a news story. Much information has been condensed for the sake of conciseness, and this creates long and complex noun groups, where nouns are preceded by adjectives or adverbs, or followed by prepositional phrases. However, the sentences tend to have a simple grammatical structure of subject + predicate + object and/or object of a preposition (only noun groups of more than two words are underlined).

Cancelled flights and baggage chaos mar Terminal 5 opening[1]
(www.thetimes.co.uk, March 27, 2008)

1 Heathrow Terminal 5's first morning open for business descended into chaos today with at least 20 flights cancelled amid huge baggage-collection delays and a host of other problems.
2 Passengers arriving at the £4.3 billion terminal faced hours of waiting as they tried to collect their luggage, after a sophisticated new baggage handling system broke down.
3 Baggage handlers were unable to log on to the new system, which had been hailed as being capable of handling 12,000 bags an hour, after computers failed to recognize staff identities.
4 Some passengers reported having to wait for up to two and a half hours for their luggage.
5 As the backlog built up, flights to Munich, Frankfurt, Paris and Brussels as well as flights to Glasgow and Aberdeen were among those cancelled.
6 Further computer difficulties meant that there was a problem with bags on departing flights early this morning, with three flights left without luggage on board.
7 British Airways, which has exclusive use of the new terminal, said it had had 'a few minor problems'.
8 'This is not unexpected following one of the most complex and largest airport moves in history,' the company said in a statement issued at around 12.30pm.

9 'These teething problems have included car parking provision, delays in staff security screening and staff familiarization with the terminal. We have also had some luggage performance issues.

10 'These issues are being resolved; overall, customers have given us a very positive reaction to Terminal 5, which we know will be a resounding success.'

11 One of six lifts in the main terminal building was also not working properly this morning.

In the first paragraph, there are three complex noun phrases: a) *Heathrow Terminal 5's first morning open for business*; b) *20 flights cancelled* and c) *huge baggage-collection delays*. The first two show an example of post-modification, that is, an adjective or participial following the head (*open for business*; *cancelled)*. Other complex nominal structures are found in paragraphs 2, 6, 7, 8, 9, 10 and 11.

In all the instances where the long nominal groups are used, alternative formulations would be possible. For example, *Heathrow Terminal 5's first morning open for business* could be formulated as: *the first morning that Terminal 5 at Heathrow was open for business*; *huge baggage-collection delays* could be rewritten as: *there were huge delays in the collection of baggage*; *a sophisticated new baggage handling system* might be rendered as: *a system for the handling of baggage that is new and sophisticated*. These alternative formulations would enhance the readability of the text, but they would, at the same time, create a text that is less compact and stylistically effective.

7.3 Use of concise, plain language

As we saw in section 7.1, writing news in concise, clear, plain language is highly valued in journalism. But what characterises this kind of language? Although no rules are prescriptively enforced, some patterns tend to emerge.

In the first place, words that are not necessary or carry little meaning tend to be avoided. For example, in the list below, the multi-word expressions on the left can be replaced with the single words on the right with no loss of meaning and with less processing effort required of the reader.

Longer	**Shorter**
in order to	to
despite the fact that	although
in the event that	if
as a result of	because
at the present time	now
with the exception of	except
subsequent to	after

Similarly, the concepts on the left in the next list can be expressed more synthetically by the wordings on the right (which are therefore preferable).

Longer	**More synthetic**
The citizens made an application	The citizens applied
They made a decision	They decided
The senator gave approval	The senator approved
He provided the appropriate information	He informed

In the second place, expressions that may be unfamiliar to the reader tend to be avoided. Potentially obscure words include slang, jargon and words of French or Latin origin. For example, in American English, slang expressions include *bad* to mean *good*; *awesome* to mean *great*; *dope* to mean *drug*. Jargon is words or expressions that are used by, and thus familiar to, only a particular profession or group. Finally, words of Latin or French origin, and which are not part of everyday vocabulary, may be better understood only by educated people. Whatever the reason, words not likely to be familiar to the general public are avoided. The examples below show some Latinate words on the left, and preferable, more familiar words on the right (there are more examples in Chapter 9).

Latin/French Origin	**More familiar**
absurdity	foolishness
construct	build
depart	leave
necessity	need
spectacular	wonderful

There is also a tendency to avoid words that are non-specific. When possible, verbs are preferred that have a strong descriptive meaning. In the examples below, the sentences on the right are preferable to those on the left (from Lansen and Stephens 2008: 37–8).

Vague	**Preferable**
The *fast-moving* bullets went through the wall quickly	The bullets *tore* through the wall
The camper *was involved* in an accident	The camper *flipped* on its side and *burst* into flames

7.4 The passive voice

Journalists tend to use dynamic, action verbs – that is, verbs that describe things that happen or actions that are made, which evolve over time. In parallel to this tendency, there is a tendency to use the active voice rather than the passive voice. From a grammatical point of view, in the active voice, the subject is the one who *performs* the action; in the passive voice, the subject is the one who *undergoes* the action, i.e., the person or thing affected by it. There are examples of active sentences in 1 and 2 below, and of passive sentences in 3 and 4 (subjects and predicates are underlined). The sentences in 5 and 6 are the active-voice equivalents of those in 3 and 4.

1 Protesters attacked police with knives and stones
2 Police arrested the protesters.
3 Three men were killed by a suspected suicide bomber
4 A question was raised by one of the attendees
5 A suspected suicide bomber killed three men
6 One of the attendees raised a question.

The active voice is the preferred form because it allows the journalist to describe actions in a manner that is more direct and easier to understand, as it reflects the way people think and process information (i.e. by mentioning first who brings about an event, and next who is affected by it). However, there are cases in which the passive voice is used. Typically, this occurs when the performer of the action is unknown or irrelevant, as in the examples below:

1 A car was broken into last night on Laurel Road
2 The body of a woman was found about 4:40 p.m. Monday in Lake Erie
3 Office mail is now delivered twice a day.

The passive voice can also be used to purposely leave the performer of the action unspecified, a strategy that the reporter can use to avoid ascribing direct responsibility for an action to anybody in particular. So the first example below does not state explicitly who is to be blamed for the incorrect administration of the drugs to the patients. On the other hand, in the second example the active voice requires the subject of the action to be named, thus ascribing direct responsibility for the action to (in this case) the hospital staff.

1 Mistakes were made while administering drugs to the patients
2 The hospital staff made mistakes while administering drugs to the patients.

Finally, because the passive voice places the undergoer of the action in subject position, it can be used by the journalist as a strategy for organizing the text around a particular figure or topic. Thus, independently of its semantic role, the same grammatical subject can occur repeatedly in sentence-initial position over a stretch of text, creating a conceptual link between parts of the text and making it more coherent and cohesive. (And reiteration of the same theme across clauses brings unity to the story.) This strategy, often used to connect paragraphs in a news story, is exemplified in the excerpt below, where all the paragraphs begin with a subject + predicate structure (underlined in the text), most of them referring to the same person (*Zahid Masood*). In this text, the differences in the names and verbs found at the beginning of the paragraphs create stylistic variation, while the parallel repetition of the same grammatical structure (subject + predicate) makes the text cohesive, logically well structured and easy to follow.

> **Man arrested NINE years after air hostess, 19, was killed in car crash on M25**[2]
>
> - Charlotte Smoker, 19, died in hospital the day after the crash on the M25 at Kent in November 2003
> - Zahid Masood, 47, was arrested on Friday and charged with causing her death by dangerous driving
> - Masood is also charged with perverting the course of justice by giving false details to police after the crash
>
> (Kerry McDermott, www.dailymail.co.uk, November 11, 2012)

1 A man has been charged over the death of a 19-year-old air hostess nine years after she was killed in a crash on the M25.

2 Zahid Masood is accused of causing the death by dangerous driving of Charlotte Smoker, who died in hospital the day after the crash on November 3, 2003.

3 The 47-year-old, from Rochester, is also charged with perverting the course of justice by giving police false details after the road accident near junction 4 of the motorway in Kent.

4 Masood was arrested on Friday. He appeared before magistrates yesterday and was remanded in custody.

5 Miss Smoker, from Bishop Stortford, Hertfordshire, had been driving towards the Dartford Crossing in a red Fiat Cinquecento when her car hit the central reservation and then collided with another vehicle.

6 A Kent Police spokesman said: 'A man has appeared in court charged with causing the death of a teenager and giving police false details in a road traffic collision nine years ago.

7 Zahid Masood was remanded in custody when he appeared at Medway Magistrates' Court.

8 'He has been charged with causing death by dangerous driving and perverting the course of justice following the collision, in which 19-year-old air hostess Charlotte Smoker from Hertfordshire died a day later from her injuries.'

9 Masood is due to appear at Maidstone Crown Court on November 19.
10 Detective Sergeant Scott Lynch, from the Kent Police Serious Collision Investigation Unit, said: 'This collision may have occurred nine years ago but we have been actively investigating it throughout that time.
11 'I would like to urge anyone who did not come forward at the time and remembers the collision to come forward now.
12 'They still may hold vital information. Call Kent Police's witness line on 01622 798538 quoting reference YY/007673/12.'

7.5 Use of syntax

In a text, syntax creates meaning. This is because the ordering of the elements in a clause determines the interpretation/assignment of the syntactic-semantic role played by the participants in the process represented in the clause. In addition, the ordering of constituents can highlight or marginalize the presence and participation of event participants. Verbs denote an action, process or state, and thus indicate the participants' degree and type of involvement in that event or situation.

In linguistics theory, for the most common verbal structure – i.e. the one involving transitive verbs, which have two arguments – a distinction is made between two kinds of participants:

- the **agent**, who actively brings about the event represented in the predicate, and so is consciously and deliberately involved in the realization of the process;
- the **affected**, that is, someone or something that undergoes the action or process expressed by the verb.
- Besides the prototypical agent, there is a similar semantic role that can be assigned to the main participant in the event, whom I will call the '**actor**': the referent or subject of an active verb, but who has a less direct, less complete and less 'causative' involvement in it. This is the role of the participant who experiences an emotion (e.g. 'Mary feels satisfied') or embodies a property ('Mary is a genius; Mary is phenomenal').

Besides the above main roles, additional arguments may be mentioned in the clause, such as the **goal**, which indicates the end-point or target of the action expressed by the verb, and the **circumstance**, which describes the time, location or situation in which the action takes place.

Some examples are shown below. We can see that examples 4–6 differ from 1–3 because they lack an affected. In addition, the last two examples express an experience or a state more than a real action.

1 John hits the ball (Agent – Process – Affected)
2 The Parliament issued the law (Agent – Process – Affected)

3 I'm preparing my speech for the convention tomorrow (Agent – Process Affected – Goal – Circumstance)
4 Susan went home (Agent – Process)
5 The children looked sad (Actor – Process)
6 The children are quiet (Actor – Process)

The reason why this is relevant here is that, by choosing different ways of expressing relations between verbs and participants, writers can present a story from different angles and can shift the focus of attention onto or away from the agent or the affected in the event described in the story. Thus, syntactic choices can be used to convey a point of view. For example, a person can be presented as the performer or the undergoer of an action, the initiator or the target, the perpetrator or the victim. Similarly, an event can be represented by placing emphasis on the action itself or on the resulting state of the process. We will now look at how this can be achieved through the choice of verbs and verb constructions.

7.5.1 Action and relational verbs

A distinction can be made between action and relational verbs. **Action verbs** express actions, while **relational** verbs express the relationships between entities. Action verbs can further be divided into **transitive** verbs, which involve an agent and an affected, and **intransitive** verbs, which only indicate that a participant – in fact, one participant – is directly involved in the process being represented. Transitive constructions express the notion that an activity is transferred from an agent to an affected, but intransitive verbs do not involve an affected. Looking at the examples above, 1–3 are transitive verbs, and 4 is intransitive.

Transitive action verbs encode the idea that the agent performs an action that has an effect on the affected. Because transitive action verbs link the subject directly and unambiguously to the action expressed by the verb, they have the effect of attributing direct responsibility for actions to them. This is shown in the examples (1) and (2) below.

1 **Robber kills NYC jewelry store worker**
(www.msnbc.msn.com, January 27, 2010)

2 **Police in California arrest man in friend's gun death**
(www.huffingtonpost.com, October 29, 2012)

In the active voice, transitive action verbs directly represent the main participant involved in the process as the one who is responsible for bringing it about. So transitive action verbs may be used to express blame. For example, in the next example the article points clearly at the police's responsibility in the shooting of the dog and implies, albeit in a veiled manner, that the action was cruel and unnecessary – suggested by the presence of words like *horrified* (*onlookers*), *apparently* (*snapped*), *sad* (*scene*). In so doing, the journalist interprets the possible reaction of the readership on the basis of the national concern about cruelty to animals.

> **Police shoot dog on busy NYC street in front of horrified onlookers**
> A New York City police officer shot a dog who apparently snapped at him in a sad scene on a busy Manhattan street.
> (www.dailymail.co.uk, August 14, 2012)

When journalists do not want to link the agent directly to the action, an alternative strategy consists in using an inanimate entity as the subject, so that the process becomes depersonalized, and the relationship between the action and the performer becomes more indirect. This is shown in the two examples below: in the first, the agent is the *bomb*, and no mention is made of the person who laid it, possibly because the attack was anonymous. In the second, the agent of the predicate *destroys* is the abstract noun *construction*. This, by objectifying the agent, obscures the responsibility of the actual people who are destroying the villagers' livelihood.

> **Bomb rocks Damascus as peace envoy meets with Assad**
> (www.latimes.com, October 21, 2012)

> **New construction on gas pipeline destroys villager's livelihoods in Mon State**
> Mudon Township residents have reported the destruction of their land due to new construction of the gas pipeline from Kanbauk to Myaingkalay.
> (monnews.org, March 22, 2011)

Another strategy that can be used to avoid suggesting blame, or when the action reported might be controversial, is to place emphasis on the victims and avoid any direct reference to the agency of the action. This can be done by using intransitive verbs. Intransitive verbs express a process in which there is no affected, and so represent events as if they had no external cause. For example, in 1 below there is no direct mention of the police's responsibility in the killing of the terror leaders. In the headline, the choice of the verb *die* represents leaders as experiencers of an event, not as undergoers of an action carried out by others; the text adds that it was the police who crushed the prison revolt, but the relationship between the leaders' death and the crushing of the revolt is left implicit and unspecified. In the lead, the verb *kill* is chosen over the verb *die* (*Leaders of a guerrilla group ... were killed*), however the agent of the killing (*police*) has been removed from this clause, only to be introduced in the following subordinate clause, where *police* is the agent of an action carried out on an abstract entity (*revolt*), rather than on people (*terror leaders*). Similarly, in 2, the news focuses on the man's death, while the fact that the Greek anti-austerity demonstration turned violent is downplayed. The man's death is not, grammatically, presented as an effect of the violence breaking out. Violence itself is presented as an event that happens of its own accord during the demonstrations, for which no explicit blame is apportioned. In 3, both clauses have an intransitive verb. In the first clause, the Arctic sea ice is viewed as 'vanishing' by itself, as a natural event for which no explanation is provided. In the second clause, *oil rigs* are personified and initiate the action of 'moving in'. In this whole scene, the human agent is implied, and the direct blame on his/her actions is removed from the reader's attention.

1 **Terror leaders die as prison revolt is crushed by police**
Leaders of a guerrilla group that has abducted and murdered scores of hostages were killed yesterday when Filipino police suppressed a bloody revolt in a maximum security prison.

(*The Times*, March 16, 2005)

2 **Man dies as violence breaks out at Greek anti-austerity demonstration**

(www.independent.co.uk, October 23, 2012)

3 **Arctic sea ice vanishes – and the oil rigs move in**

(science.time.com, September 11, 2012)

Relational verbs express states of 'being' or 'having', or set up relationships between one thing and another, or between an actor and a quality or attribute of theirs. Two examples of relational verbs are given in 5 and 6 (section 7.5) above. Other relational verbs are:

represent	indicate	manifest
show	express	need
reflect	become	mean
exemplify	reveal	

Relational verbs are used frequently in news reporting, and particularly in hard news, to present qualities or attributes of people and objects. Relational verbs like *be*, *show*, *represent*, *mean*, *reveal* position readers to view the reported events as objective truths, and make sentences difficult to contest. Thus, they can be a powerful and persuasive tool in the journalist's hands. In the next two examples the newspaper's opinion is presented as a fact that cannot be challenged.

1 **Qatar ruler's visit is major boost for Hamas**
(www.belfasttelegraph.co.uk, October 23, 2012)

2 **China manufacturing shows signs of recovery**
(the *West Australian*, October 24, 2012).

7.5.2 Use of voice and thematization

Another way in which syntactic choices may affect the presentation of participants involved in the story is through the use of **voice**. As seen in section 7.4, active and passive voice forms offer different ways of encoding the agent of the verbal process in the sentence structure: while in active constructions the agent and the grammatical subject of the verb coincide, in passive constructions the grammatical subject is the affected of the verbal process. Compare the two following sentences (grammatical subjects and verbs are underlined):

1 Police detain 93 asylum seekers
2 93 asylum seekers are detained by police

The two sentences mean the same thing, but their focus is different. Sentence 1 is about *police*; 2 is about *93 asylum seekers*. This is because in English the grammatical subject is normally the same as the topic (or **theme**) of the sentence, that is, what is being talked about. Thus, whatever is placed in initial position in a sentence is emphasized. After the topic, usually occurring at the beginning of each sentence, the rest of the sentence, the **rheme**, tells the reader something about the theme.

Using the passive voice inverts the order of the elements in the sentence and so reverses the relation between theme and rheme. As we saw in section 7.4, this may be done for stylistic reasons. However, the passive voice can also be used purposely to avoid mentioning the agent. In 3, the agent that was explicit in 1 and 2 is omitted, resulting in a more vague and indefinite presentation of the event:

3 93 asylum seekers are detained.

When the agent is not mentioned, the effect is that the responsibility of the action is depersonalized and obfuscated: 'When Agents are deleted there can be the impression that the process erupts spontaneously into the world. Deletion can serve the purposes of economy and/or distortion' (Conboy 2007: 61).

An example of how the choice of voice and subject thematization may have significant implications for the preferred reading of the news is given by comparing the headlines and leads of two stories dealing with a pro-Tibet rally held in China involving monks, nuns and Tibetans, and which ended in violence.

1 **Paramilitaries open fire on hundreds of monks and nuns at Tibet rally**
Paramilitary police opened fire on hundreds of monks, nuns and Tibetans who tried to march on a local government office in western China yesterday to demand the return of the Dalai Lama.
(www.thetimes.co.uk, March 25, 2008)

2 **Two killed at pro-Tibet rally in China**
A police officer and a Tibetan monk were killed in Sichuan province, southern China, it was reported today, after another Tibetan independence demonstration turned violent. [...]
(www.guardian.co.uk, March 25, 2008)

The Times headline, 'Paramilitaries open fire on hundreds of monks and nuns at Tibet rally', is written in the active voice. It specifies that the agents of the predicate *open fire* are the *paramilitaries*, and the affected (the receivers of the *open fire* action) are *hundreds of monks and nuns*. The headline thereby places the full responsibility for the action on the paramilitaries. On the other hand, the affected appears as a mass of harmless people (*hundreds of monks and nuns*). The text of the lead implies that blame for the violent outcome of the demonstration is attributable to the *paramilitary police*, the subject of the predicate *open fire*. By contrast, the group of monks, nuns and Tibetans are the subject of two verbs that express inability to act (*tried to march*) and an oral activity (*demanded the return*).

In the extract from the *Guardian*, the headline uses a passive construction (*Two killed*), in which the grammatical subject is unspecified (*two*) and the agent is omitted. In the lead, the text says that both *a police officer* and *a monk* were killed, emphasizing that victims were reported on both sides of the fight. In addition, the article makes an abstract, impersonal reference to the monks and nuns' protest, calling it *Tibetan independence demonstration*. This abstract entity is the subject of the action verb *turned violent*, which obscures the responsibility for the violence it expresses. As a result of using these strategies, the article from the *Guardian* appears more neutral, presenting a situation where no single person is to blame, while *The Times* appears to side with the victims.

7.6 An example: describing victims through verb choice and verbal constructions

The following article shows how verb choices and verbal constructions can help to describe victims in a story.

In Ghana's witch camps, the accused are never safe[3]
Ghana has pledged to close its camps where women accused of witchcraft are detained for years. But the women might not be safe back in their communities.

(Robyn Dixon, *Los Angeles Times*, September 9, 2012)

1 JOHANNESBURG, South Africa – In the witch camps of Ghana, the dying contortions of a slaughtered chicken determine the guilt of an accused woman: witch, or not.

2 If the chicken falls with its head down and its feet in the air, the woman is declared a witch and she must spend the rest of her days in the squalor of the camp, abandoned by her family, with just one unfortunate young relation sent by her family to care for her until she dies.

3 And if the chicken collapses feet down and she's declared innocent of witchcraft? She still must spend her remaining years in the camp, just in case some villagers don't believe in her innocence.

4 'They're not safe when they return,' said Adwoa Kwateng-Kluvitse, Ghana director for international aid organization Action Aid, which is working to educate northern Ghanaian communities on the rights of the accused in an effort to end witchcraft accusations.

5 'Even if the ritual says she's innocent, there will be members of the community who will feel unsafe.'

6 Northern Ghana has six witch camps that have been in existence for more than 100 years, accommodating 800 accused witches – almost all of them women – and 500 relatives sent by families to take care of them.

7 Last year, the Ghanaian government announced that the witch camps must be closed in 2012. But that will be no easy task because of the stigma attached to the women.

8 The camps are places of shame, from which there is almost never an escape. Elderly women, often widows, are accused when something goes wrong: a drowned child, an outbreak of malaria, a drought, a spate of cattle deaths, or something as simple as a cow trying to jump a fence and knocking it down. Some are accused merely because someone dreamed about them.

9 After the chicken slaughter ritual, they're often forced to drink a cleansing potion consisting of chicken blood and dirt.

10 'The witch camps are effectively women's prisons where inmates have been given no trial, have no right of appeal but have received a life sentence,' said a recent report by Action Aid.

11 'The typical story is that there will be allegations, and emotions rise,' Kwateng-Kluvitse said in a phone interview. 'In some cases, the woman hears about it and flees. But often they're caught and brutalized. Usually it's the young men in the community who brutalize them, shoving them, pushing them, beating them. Some of them are killed.'

12 In 2010, a 78-year-old woman was accused of witchcraft in the town of Tema and set afire by three women and two men, including a pastor, in a case condemned by authorities.
13 Sano Kojo has been living in a camp for 30 years, since she was in her mid-30s and accused of killing her cousin by pressing on his chest.
14 'Once you are here, you are forgotten,' she said, according to the report.
15 Asana, 27, whose last name wasn't supplied in the report, was pregnant when she was accused by her husband, who dreamed she wanted to kill him. She ended up in a witch camp called Gambaga.
16 'One day when I was five months pregnant, while I was in the fields with other women, he came after me and he beat me with no mercy. While I was on the ground he took out a knife. The other women were begging him to stop.
17 'He did not kill me at the end. I was taken to a shrine,' she said, referring to a place at the witch camp where accusations of witchcraft are tested. 'There, he melted plastic and poured it on my body. When I came here my whole body was in terrible pain.'
18 Families typically send a young relation, usually a granddaughter or great-granddaughter age 10 to 14, to look after the accused, cook, collect firewood and water, and clean.
19 The girls also become tainted by the witch camps, drop out of school and can't go back to their families even after the death of the relation they are sent to care for. Some of these once-young women have been in the camp for 40 years.
20 'It's an abuse of the rights of the children in the camps. It affects their rights to education, to play and live with their families,' Kwateng-Kluvitse said.
21 Kwateng-Kluvitse said that although her organization supported the eventual closure of the camps, it was important to do so gradually, only after community attitudes were changed and women could live safely in communities without fear of being accused anew.
22 Action Aid would not advocate just dismantling the camps overnight,' she said. 'Where would women go; where they could be safe? It has to be a process.'
23 She said it could take 10 or 20 years before the camps could be shut down for good because of the strong resistance in the accusing communities.
24 It's something that they have believed in for generations,' she said. 'The idea of witchcraft had never been challenged, and there are some people with entrenched views.'

The article discusses what happens to women in Ghana who are believed to be witches. They are abandoned by their families, expelled from their villages, and sent to detention camps where they stay until their death. It would be hard to dispute that the treatment of these women is unfair or that they pay a high price for something they did not do. Thus the story assumes a consensus with the readership that Ghanaian women accused of witchcraft are victims of an unjust tradition. They are viewed as powerless beings, doomed to a fate they do not even try to change.

In the story the women are presented mainly as subjects of passive constructions, where they undergo actions imposed on them by others: *they are accused of witchcraft*; *they are detained for years*; *the woman is declared...*; *they are often forced...*; *they have been given no trial*; *they're caught and brutalized*; *Some of them are killed*; *a 78-year-old woman was set afire*; *you are forgotten*; *I was taken to a shrine*; *The girls also become tainted*; *they are sent....* They are often presented as subjects and actors of relational verbs, which express states and not actions: *are never safe*; *they have no right of appeal*; *she was in her mid-30s*; *she was pregnant*; *she was in the field*; *she was on the ground*. When they are agents of action verbs, these are mostly intransitive verbs – that is, their actions have no effect on other people or things: *they return*; *the woman hears about it and flees*; *Sano Kojo has been living*; *she ended up in a camp*; *I came here*; *[they] drop out of school and can't go back*; *women could live*; *women go*. In a few cases, the women are agents of action verbs, but these relate to abstractions – their actions have no physical impact on other people or things: *must spend the rest of her days*; *have received a life sentence*; *she said*; *The other women were begging him to stop*.

The story does not clearly point an accusatory finger at anyone, as if the real agent acting against the women was a broad and widespread phenomenon that is above the single individuals. Most passive constructions have omitted agents (*the woman is declared*; *Elderly women ... are accused*; *... accused merely because someone dreamed*; *they're often forced to drink*). Other participants in the story are Ghana (*Ghana has pledged to close its camps*; *Northern Ghana has six witch camps*; *Ghanaian government announced that the witch camps must be closed*), and unspecified subjects (*some villagers don't believe in her innocence*; *someone dreamed about them; there will be allegations, and emotions rise*). When people are indeed mentioned as agents of the actions that affect the women's fate these are mostly men, performing action verbs. However, this occurs starting with paragraph 11: *it's the young men in the community who brutalize them, shoving them, pushing them, beating them*; *was set afire by three women and two men, including a pastor*; *he beat me with no mercy*; *he took out a knife*; *he melted plastic and poured it on my body*.

Here we have examined some linguistic strategies that can be used to highlight information and convey a point of view. In the next chapter we will look at how points of view can be conveyed via strategies for reporting speech and expressing modality.

Students' activities

Activity 1

An exercise on nominalizations in headlines.

Look at the headlines below. In each headline:

- Underline all the nominalized forms. For each nominal form, write down the corresponding verb.
- Rewrite the headline de-nominalizing the nominalized form (e.g., *Zoo welcomes arrival of baby tapir* → *Zoo welcomes the baby tapir that has arrived*). Reflect on how nominalizations allow for the creation of highly synthetic headlines.

USA faces critical adoption shortage
(*USA Today Weekend*, January 11–13, 2013)

Bangkok candidate denies wrongdoing
(the *Wall Street Journal*, January 10, 2013)

School overcrowding soars to record level
(*Daily Mail*, October 26, 2010)

Helicopter horror crash
(*London Evening Standard*, January 17, 2013)

Taking action on guns
(the *Philadelphia Inquirer*, January 17, 2013)

Agreement ends bus disruptions
(*Times Colonist*, January 17, 2013)

L.A. pension boards asked to end investments in assault gun firms
(www.latimes.com, January 17, 2013)

International court launches investigation of Mali abuses
(www.latimes.com, January 17, 2013)

Admiration for a citizen standing up to power
(www.newssun.com, January 16, 2013)

Activity 2

An exercise on the use of complex noun groups in headlines.

The following headlines contain complex noun groups. 'Unpack' them and rewrite the headlines to make their informative content less compact and easier to process (e.g., *night safe ride bike light* → *A night light for bikes that makes riding safe*).

Pipe-bomb suspect arrested in Nevada
(Associated Press, May 8, 2002)

Former Bears coach Ditka suffers stroke
(Reuters, November 16, 2012)

Arabian archaeology exhibition unveiled
(www.usatoday.com, November 16, 2012)

12-son football dynasty
(www.cbsnews.com, November 16, 2012)

New Guinness record holders
(www.cnn.com, November 16, 2012)

Controversy over new fat-fighting soda
(www.cnn.com, November 16, 2012)

Children's PeaPod travel beds recalled
(www.webmd.com, November 16, 2012)

Activity 3

Access *The Times in Plain English* at: www.thetimesinplainenglish.com/wp. This site collects stories written in plain English: a form of English that is more easily 'processable' than news English, because it does not make use of features that may hinder comprehensibility, such as complex noun groups. Read some of the stories in this site. How do they differ from the stories written in a more standard news reporting style?

Activity 4

Analyse the two headlines and leads below. Compare the difference in the perspective conveyed by the two articles, as it is expressed through the linguistic choices made in the headlines and leads. Explain it by making reference to the use of subject thematization and choice of active or passive verbs.

I. **Irish riot police attack students after they occupy Department of Finance in Dublin**
Riot police attacked students in Dublin Weds Nov 3rd with dogs, armoured vehicles and horses after the students protesting against government cuts occupied the Department of Finance and threw eggs at the Dail.
(www.wsm.ie, November 3, 2010)

II. **Gardaí students clash in Dublin**
Student leaders have condemned the action of protestors who clashed with Gardaí [Irish Peace Guardians] after a protest against plans to increase registration fees for third level students.
(www.rte.ie, November 3, 2010)

Activity 5

Find other examples, from online or print papers, of how differences in perspectives are conveyed through the use of subject thematization and choice of voice.

Further reading

Fairclough, N. 2000. *New Labour, New Language?* London and New York, Routledge.
Hodge, R., and Kress, G. 1993. *Language as Ideology*, London and New York, Routledge.
Knapp, P., and Watkins, M. 2005. *Genre, Text, Grammar: Technologies for Teaching and Assessing Writing*, Sidney, University of New South Wales Press.
Pape, S., and Featherstone, S. 2005. *Newspaper Journalism: A Practical Introduction*, London, Sage.
Reah, D. 2002. *The Language of Newspapers*, London and New York, Routledge.
Simpson, P. 1993. *Language, Ideology and Point of View*, London and New York, Routledge.

Chapter 8

Reporting information and evaluating likelihood

This chapter discusses how journalists use direct and indirect quotes or paraphrases to report sources' words and to convey a slant on events. It also discusses the use of modality as a way to encode the degree to which the reported events are viewed as possible, likely, necessary or desirable.

8.1 Encoding attitude and point of view

News stories represent the outcome of a series of linguistic choices which reflect journalists' individual views of the world and their desire to create consensus with their readers. We have seen how the choice of verbs and sentence structures allows the journalist to highlight information to shift the readers' attention onto or away from the agent of an event reported in his/her story. Now we examine how using different reporting structures and expressions of modality allows journalists not to endorse what the source has said, or to hint at their reservations about the truthfulness or likelihood of the reported event.

8.2 Use of reported speech

As we saw in Chapter 3, journalists learn to create coherent stories by embedding or reworking material from various sources. Reporting speech is a particularly frequent feature of news language, and one in which skilled journalists distinguish themselves. They can make use of the linguistic structures for reporting speech that are available in the language to draw attention to, or deflect it away from, parts of the information contained in the sources' words. These structures can be used either to emphasize emotional and dramatic content and create an impact on the readership or to de-emphasize information that may be controversial or not well received.

The two basic structures for reporting speech in English are **direct speech** and **indirect speech**. The choice between these two structures relates to different principles of representing verbal processes: the idealized function of direct speech is to report speech in a manner true to its original wording;

the function of indirect speech is to report what was said, but with wording that can be different from the original.

These basic principles are observed also in news writing, with the two structures giving the journalist different degrees of flexibility in reporting the sources' words. When **direct quotes** are used, the assumption is that the journalist is reporting the source's words exactly. With **indirect quotes**, the journalist may not adhere strictly to the source's words, although those used may actually be fairly close to the original ones. A third option is to report the source's words through a **paraphrase**, which gives the gist of what the source said, but in words that may be quite different from the original. Finally, journalists may use a mixture of paraphrase and quotes, which may serve the need to emphasize a few words out of a quote that is not deemed particularly interesting (see also Chapter 3).

The following examples (from a story about an 8-year-old boy charged with killing two) show different ways of reporting the same piece of information. In (1), the defence attorney's words are reported in quotes; in (2), the words are reported with an indirect quote, that is, they are embedded in the paragraph; in (3), the words of the police are paraphrased; in (4), some of the words spoken by the Police Chief are reported in quotes, the others are summarized in a paraphrase.

1 **Direct Quote**
'They became very accusing early on in the interview,' Brewer said. 'Two officers with guns at their sides, it's very scary for anybody, for sure an 8-year-old kid.'
(www.cnn.com, November 7, 2008)

2 **Indirect Quote**
One of his defense attorneys said he was not read his rights and did not have an attorney or a parent present during questioning and said that was improper.
(www.cnn.com, November 18, 2008)

3 **Paraphrase**
Police have not responded to those claims.
(www.cnn.com, November 18, 2008)

4 **Quote and Paraphrase**
[St Johns Police Chief Roy] Melnick said the boy didn't act on the 'spur of the moment,' though he didn't elaborate further.
(adapted from www.nydailynews.com, November 8, 2008)

8.2.1 *Choosing between different ways of reporting speech*

How do reporters choose how to report the source's words? Choosing between quotes and paraphrases is not done randomly. Their use has different purposes. In general, **direct quotes** allow the journalist to 'add a voice' to the reported story (i.e., they use the words uttered by the people in the story). This gives a dialogic dimension to the news and has the effect of increasing the immediacy and vividness of the story. Through their spoken words, the people in the story become alive to the reader as they tell their feelings, reactions and opinions. A story that is more personal also becomes more involving, because quotes increase its narrative potential, and let the reader relate directly with the person whose words are reported.

In the example below the personality of Miss Universe is brought to life by her words (in paragraphs 1 and 2), giving voice to her love and pride for her country in the moment of her triumph: '*I want the whole world to know about my country and my people*'; '*I imagine that they're all going crazy in Mexico right now*'; '*I'm extremely proud and I'm sure they're very proud, too*'. In her words, the use of plain, informal English narrows the distance with the reader. Her words are then added value to by the quote of Mexican President Felipe Calderon, who echoes her and also talks, in a more formal language, about the Mexicans being proud of her victory.

Mexico's newest icon: 22-year-old Miss Universe[1]
(Oskar Garcia, Associated Press, August 24, 2010)

1 LAS VEGAS (AP) - From flags to Facebook, 22-year-old Jimena Navarrete has quickly made it clear what she plans to promote as the world's newest Miss Universe – her home country of Mexico.

2 'I want the whole world to know about my country and my people,' the Guadalajara native said after beating 82 competitors for global bragging rights at the pageant in Las Vegas.

3 'I imagine that they're all going crazy in Mexico right now,' she said through an interpreter. 'I'm extremely proud and I'm sure they're very proud, too.'

4 She donned a flowing red dress, strutted confidently in a violet bikini, and said onstage that the Internet is indispensable and requires parents to impart family values.

5 The model-turned pageant queen then posed for pictures with a Mexican flag and Mexico's last Miss Universe as congratulations from her countrymen came pouring in.

6 'Her triumph is a source of pride and satisfaction for all Mexicans, who see in her the fruits of perseverance,' Mexican President Felipe Calderon said in a statement. Immediately after her win, Calderon said on Twitter that her victory would help Mexico's image as a country.

7 'We won, long live Mexico!' Navarrete said on her fan page on Facebook, spurring 478 'likes' and 218 comments in about one hour.
8 She was cheered by Spanish-speaking reporters clamoring to talk with her after the pageant, and twice answered questions about Arizona's recent immigration law.
[...]

Like direct quotes, **indirect quotes** allow reporters to add information that is credible and authentic by virtue of coming from an attributed source. However, the use of indirect quotes allows the writer to reproduce the source's opinions without using their exact words. This can be useful when the reporter wants to focus not on making the speaker come alive to the reader but on reporting the substance of what he/she said. The use of indirect quotes also allows the reporter to control the information, giving him/her the flexibility to combine, move or omit parts of the source's speech, and emphasize the parts that are of interest. Thus, because an indirect quote may not always be distinguishable from the narration, it may be suitable for use when the information reported could be considered controversial, or when the reporter does not want to draw attention to some parts of the source's speech.

Often, indirect quotes can be used to introduce a speaker and a situation, with direct quotes then used in what follows to report the speaker's views on the event. In other words, indirect quotes can provide the narrative and prepare the reader for the direct quotation, thus functioning as a transition into the story. Here is an example:

> Konigsmark said he was in the home when suddenly, around 7:45 p.m., the whole house shook with what sounded like a bomb going off on the bottom floor.
>
> 'That was the craziest thing that ever happened,' Konigsmark said as he stood, dazed, outside the wreckage of his house.
>
> (adapted from: www.sfgate.com, November 17, 2008)

Quotes are not essential to reporting a story. Most of the times, a good reporter can get the point across more clearly with a well-attributed paraphrase, without quotation marks. **Paraphrases** are used when the source's words are not particularly dramatic, interesting or clear, or when they are difficult for the readership to understand (for example in the case of government reports), grammatically incorrect, or too colloquial to look good in writing.

Being able to ring the changes on quotes and paraphrases gives reporters a good deal of stylistic flexibility. In the Miss Universe story above, paragraph 4 provides an alternative to the direct quotes in paragraphs 2, 3 and 6. The use of different types of structure makes the text less repetitive and more enjoyable to read. In addition, because the type of quote selected allows journalists to emphasize or downplay particular aspects of the sources' voices, reporting speech can be used as a strategy for conveying a journalistic angle.

8.2.2 Other functions of reported speech

As seen in Chapter 3, using quotes from different sources allows journalists to present an objective account of the events, in which the voice of the reporter is not explicitly expressed.

Direct quotes can be used by reporters to give authority to a statement, or to emphasize that a particular word or phrase represents the source's and not the journalist's opinion. This may be necessary, for example, when the article reports surprising and uncommon facts, or exceptional findings and discoveries. In the example below the report of the discovery of the monkey is accompanied by quotes commenting on its colours ('*is unlike anything I've ever seen*'; '*It's really pretty spectacular*'). Their function is to validate the fact that the monkey does have truly exceptional colours. Such comments might appear frivolous if expressed by the journalist or a layperson, but they acquire value when uttered by an expert in the field, whose position is identified by an attribution. In addition, by using quotes, the journalist can report the researcher's colloquial, emphatic expressions that would not be suited to the formal, detached, objective style typical of news language. Reported in quotes, though, Dr Hart's informal language is acceptable.

> Scientists have identified a new species of African monkey whose coloring 'is unlike anything I've ever seen,' as a researcher put it.
>
> [...]
>
> 'It's really pretty spectacular,' said John Hart, the researcher who described the coloring. Dr Hart is a scientist with the Lukuru Foundation, a wildlife research group.
>
> (adapted from: www.nytimes.com, September 13, 2012)

Direct quotes can also be used by reporters to distance themselves from the truthfulness of a certain statement. Quotes can work as a disowning device, allowing the journalist to report what the source has said without endorsing it. Here are two instances:

> **Perry says Corsicana man a 'monster'**
>
> (www.chron.com, October 15, 2009)

> Italian Prime Minister Silvio Berlusconi, on an official visit to Russia, described US President-elect Barack Obama as 'young, handsome and even suntanned.'
>
> (www.upi.com, November 6, 2008)

In the first example the word *monster* is in quotes. These have the function of showing that the word was actually uttered by *Perry*, and not by the journalist; also, their use means that the journalist is not committing to the truthfulness or appropriateness of the word in quotes, and so cannot be blamed for using a derogatory word to name the Corsicana man. Similarly, the second example reports the words used by former Italian Prime Minister Berlusconi to describe the newly elected US President Obama. The words *young, handsome and even suntanned* – definitely not appropriate to refer to a President – are presented by the journalist in quotes to emphasize that they were uttered by the Italian Prime Minister, and so he can be blamed for them.

As these examples show, using quotes allows journalists to justify the presence of words or expressions that would violate the journalistic principles of objectivity and fairness. If they put it in quotes, journalists can also use language that would not be considered appropriate (because colloquial, slang, etc.) in a news story. As with all linguistic choices, the reporter's decision on what parts of the source's speech to report, and in what order, both reflects his or her viewpoint and provides a preferred interpretation of the event.

8.3 Modality

Another linguistic strategy that can be used to introduce a personal, subjective view of the narrated event is modality.

Modality refers to the use of linguistic expressions to indicate the degree to which a fact or event is considered possible, necessary or desirable. It can be expressed with modal verbs (*can*, *will*, *shall*, *may*, *must*, *could*, *would*, *should*, *might*), but also with adverbs, such as *likely*, *undoubtedly*, *probably*, *certainly*, *conceivably*, *necessarily*, etc., and with phrases such as *it is certain that*, *it is possible that*, *it seems that*, *it appears that*. All of these encode different degrees of subjective response in the view of the speaker or writer.

Two kinds of modality are distinguished: epistemic and deontic.

Epistemic modality expresses the notions of 'speculation', 'probability', or 'certainty'. Expressions of epistemic modality indicate the degree to which speakers/writers express judgment on the truth of the propositions they utter/write. Consider the following example:

> The rising levels of congestion and air pollution found in most of the world's cities *can/may/might/could/must/will* be attributed directly to the rapidly increasing number of private cars in use.

The idea expressed here is that there is a direct relation between the rapidly increasing number of private cars in use and the rising levels of congestion and air pollution found in most of the world's cities. Changing the modal verb changes the way in which this idea is presented: with *can* it appears very possible; *may/might/could* suggest that there is a strong possibility that it is not true; *must* indicates a deduction based on the available evidence. *Will*, which is used in English as a way of expressing the future tense, conveys the idea of prediction: it indicates a strong possibility that this idea will be true in the future.

Deontic modality is concerned with the criterion by which speakers/writers decide which future events are necessary, possible, desirable, etc. Deontic modals are *must*, *should*, *may* (and *have to*).

> You *must/should/have to/may* leave now.

Here *must* expresses an order, *should* a recommendation, *have to* a necessity, and *may* a permission.

Expressions of modality are often used in news reporting because they give journalists a means of presenting affiliations and disaffections in the way they tell the events in their stories. If epistemic modality lets the writer tell readers about the certainty of occurrence of a present, past or future event, deontic modality is used when informing readers about actions that affect them – for example, when governmental decisions are made to oblige certain personnel to do something, or in commentaries in which certain directions or policies are suggested. In general, expressions of epistemic modality are more frequent than those of deontic modality, due to the inherent meanings that the expressions of modality convey.

In headlines, modals may be used to present the particular angle that will then be developed in the story. Because their use affects the way news is conceptualized and interpreted by the readership, reporters are careful to distinguish between internal and external points of view. This is particularly true with deontic modality, which relates to how verbal processes may affect readers. Consider the following examples.

1 **Nuclear operators must act now on safety: EU**
Regulators and operators should act now to improve safety at nuclear power plants, the EU energy commissioner said on Thursday, following inspections across the European Union.
(www.reuters.com, October 4, 2012)

2 **Prisoners will not get the vote, says David Cameron**
Britain will continue to defy a European Court ruling saying prisoners must be given the right to vote, Prime Minister David Cameron has said.
(www.bbc.co.uk, October 24, 2012)

3 **Catholic church in France may become mosque**
A church in the central French town of Vierzon may be converted to a mosque, as Muslims across Europe are converting empty churches to fit their faith – but some locals are worried about the threat of radicalism.
(rt.com, October 12, 2012)

4 **7 Foods you should never eat**
Food scientists are shedding light on items loaded with toxins and chemicals – and simple swaps for a cleaner diet and supersized health.
(www.foxnews.com, December 2, 2011)

In 1, the modal verb *must* is used to talk about a directive coming from the central authority of the European Union, imposing new rules to increase safety in the operations of nuclear power plants. Its use is acceptable in this context, and in fact *must* is regularly used to refer to a strong obligation or, as in this case, to an imposition. In addition, because the article discusses safety issues, the reporter can assume that the news will generate consensus among the readership. Even so, however, the journalist aims to distance himself from the obligation expressed by the verb and underlines that this is an external point of view by putting a colon in the headline.

Similarly, in 2, the modal verb *will* conveys a strong expression of certainty. It is used to voice the forceful words of British Prime Minister David Cameron, defying a European Court ruling aimed at giving prisoners the right to vote. In this case, too, it is possible that the issue voiced by the Prime Minister finds consensus among the British population. In any case, the reporter emphasizes the power of Cameron's words by using *will* in the headline, at the same time distancing himself from them, by presenting them as a quote.

On the other hand, the modal expressions in examples 3 and 4 do not have as strong a meaning; in both cases, the news is presented as if it could express the opinion of the reporter.

As the examples suggest, the choice of modal expressions in a story can greatly change the perspective it offers. That is why modals can be a powerful tool in reporting news. Let us now look at two stories that show how nuances of probability can be conveyed.

8.3.1 Weather forecasts

Epistemic modality is frequently found in weather forecasts, which, by their very nature, express tentative predictions. Here is a weather forecast published in the days before Hurricane Sandy hit the east coast of the US on October 29, 2012, causing major disasters in many areas, including New York City.

Hurricane Sandy could bring snow, driving rain to the New York City area[2]

(Victoria Cavaliere, www.nydailynews.com, October 25, 2012)

1 Hurricane Sandy was lashing the Caribbean on Thursday and the massive storm might have New York in its sights.

2 Sandy, the 18th named storm of the Atlantic hurricane season, could bring powerful winds, flooding, heavy rain and even snow to the tri-state region by Monday, forecasts predict.

3 It could be the second year in a row that snow has dusted the area in late October.

4 'Some computer models are saying the storm will come into the shoreline at Delaware and southern New Jersey,' said AccuWeather meteorologist Elliot Abrams.

5 'If that happens, we could have tropical storm or hurricane-force wind gusts, flooding rains and quite a bit of flooding along the coast,' he said.

6 The possibility of snow would come courtesy of an unusual hybrid of a tropical storm meeting cold air coming from the north, forecasters explain.

7 It was still far too soon to predict how the storm will impact the region, but the National Hurricane Center gave it about a 70% chance of continuing its current northward track up the Atlantic.

8 Sandy was upgraded from a tropical storm to a hurricane overnight after lashing Jamaica. Two people died, the Associated Press reported.

9 By early Thursday the storm was packing maximum sustained winds of 105 mph as it moved over eastern Cuba. The Category 2 storm passed west of Guantanamo Bay, where pre-trial hearings were being held for a suspect in the deadly 2000 attack on the US Navy destroyer Cole off Yemen, but wind gusts of 35 miles per hour were reported.

10 The storm marched north at about 20 mph and made landfall in Bahamas late Thursday, the National Hurricane Center said. Heavy rain and tropical storm conditions are predicted in Haiti, the Dominican Republic and the southeastern Florida coast.

11 Preparations for the storm are already under way in New Jersey.

12 The utility Jersey Central Power & Light, which was criticized for its response to Tropical Storm Irene in August 2011, says it has placed its employees on alert.

13 The storm could affect the tri-state region during a full moon, when tides are highest. That could increase the likelihood of flooding in coast areas.

The text is based, in large part, on the predictions of the weather forecasts. These determine the likelihood of the precipitation and other meteorological conditions connected with the arrival of Hurricane Sandy, as they are reported in the text. This likelihood is expressed with the modal verb *could* (headline, paragraphs 2, 3, 5, 13) , and by the expression *The possibility … would come* (paragraph 6). In paragraph 1, a piece of information is not attributed to the weather forecasts, and is made to appear highly tentative by the use of the modal verb *might*. In paragraph 4, the accurate predictions of the computer models are reported with the modal verb *will*, which contrasts with the meteorologist's hypothesis, expressed with *could* (paragraph 5). In paragraph 7, *will* is used to indicate a prediction in the future. Finally, in paragraphs 8–13, the events that have already occurred in relation to the hurricane, and thus are real, are described with no modal verbs.

8.3.2 When the news is uncertain . . .

Modal expressions are also often used when the reported news is vague or uncertain. In Chapter 3 (section 3.4.2), the story 'Airstrike may have killed Saddam' was used in discussing how modality can be used to express uncertainty about the reliability of reported events. It was shown that, when the news reported in the story is unreliable, this may be signalled by using several expressions of epistemic modality, combined with attributions of the information to unspecified sources.

In the case of that story the news concerned the outcomes of an air bombing during a war, and it is very possible that in such circumstances the reporter only gets partial or confused news. In other cases, the news may be uncertain or vague because there is a deliberate lack of information surrounding the story, and so the journalist is forced to draw inferences from the facts. The story reported below represents one of these.

> **Mysterious woman flanking N.K. leader highly likely to be his wife: gov't source**[3]
>
> (english.yonhapnews.co.kr, July 15, 2012)

1 SEOUL, July 15 (Yonhap) – The mysterious woman who has repeatedly been seen closely flanking North Korean leader Kim Jong-un in a recent series of public appearances, is highly likely to be his wife, a South Korean government source said Sunday.

2 'From the protocol point of view, such as this woman's place and table settings, it is highly likely that she's his wife and first Chairman Kim must actually be married,' the source said on condition of anonymity, referring to Kim's title as first chairman of the powerful National Defense Commission.

3 The unidentified woman first appeared in state media on July 5 when she was seen seated right next to the leader during a music concert. Analysts said at the time she might be either Kim's wife or a younger sister.

4 The stylish-looking woman was seen again on July 8 paying tribute to late North Korean founder Kim Il-sung, bowing deeply while standing next to the leader, as uniformed North Korean military officials raised their hands in salute behind the couple dressed in black.
5 On Sunday, the North's state TV released footage showing Kim bending over to talk to children during the kindergarten visit as the woman, clad in a yellow polka dot dress and a luxurious-looking white cardigan with a stylish hairstyle and high-heeled shoes, looked on next to him.
6 North Korean officials accompanying the leader were seen standing a few steps behind them.
7 State media did not identify who she was, but her act was seen as that of a first lady.
8 Few personal details are known about the young North Korean leader, including his marital status and exact age, except that he studied in Switzerland when he was young. Kim assumed control of the communist nation after his father Kim Jong-il died in December.
9 Cheong Seong-chang, a senior fellow at the Sejong Institute, said the woman appears to be Kim's wife, and the North appears to be releasing the images of her to dispel any misgivings among the North Korean public that their leader is too young.

The story is about a woman seen accompanying the recently declared supreme leader of North Korea, Kim Jong-Un, following the death of his father Kim Jong-il in December 2011. Because of the Kim family's secretive management style, little was known about Kim Jong-Un before he was declared leader, and even afterwards many details about his personal life were not known. When he first appeared in public with a younger, elegant lady, observers wondered whether she was his wife or sister. When she was then seen with him at various public events, this led to much public speculation about her identity, which finally ended when Kim Jong-Un announced she was his wife.

The story above is centred on the 'mystery' of the unknown woman flanking Kim Jong-Un: she is referred to as *mysterious woman*; *unidentified woman*; *the woman*; . . . *did not identify who she was*. However, the article of July 15 projects a strong possibility that the woman is Kim Jong-Un's wife (*highly likely to be his wife*, headline and paragraph 1). The speculation is based on hypotheses and logical conclusions, which are expressed respectively through the modal forms *highly likely* and *must*. On July 5, on the other hand, on her first appearance in public, the possibility that the young woman was Kim Jong-Un's wife was much less probable (*Analysts said at the time she* might be *either Kim's wife or a younger sister*). And because the matter, relating to Kim Jong-Un's personal life, is very sensitive in view of his importance for the state of North Korea, sources prefer to remain anonymous – *the source said on condition of anonymity* (paragraph 2); *Analysts said*; *State media*) – and are not attributed. The only attribution is found in paragraph 9, which quotes a South Korean think tank, a source that is distant from Kim Jong-Un (*Cheong Seong-chang, a senior fellow at the Sejong Institute, said*).

As this example shows, expressions of epistemic modality are a useful tool to convey tentativeness and speculation in a news story.

Students' activities

Activity 1

The last two examples in section 8.2.2 above, and Nos 1 and 2 in section 8.3, show that, when the reported information is considered potentially controversial, headlines may contain a quote or indicate the source of information. Indeed, the use of quotes in headlines allows reporters not to get the blame for what they report. This strategy also lets journalists use expressions that would otherwise not be considered appropriate in news headlines because they may be slang, may carry emotional meaning, or – as in the case of deontic modality – may appear too forceful.

Look for headlines, from print or online papers, which contain quotes or show attribution of information, explain the strategy used, and give the reasons for using it.

Activity 2

Analyse two articles reporting on the same event. In each article make a note of the following:

- What sources are being quoted?
- Are sources being quoted that express opposing viewpoints?
- Are there more quotes or interviews about only one side of the issue?
- Is the reporter challenging the viewpoints expressed by the sources?
- Are there anonymous sources?
- Is there any information that is given as shared information and is not attributed?

Activity 3

Choose a couple of stories from this book: for example, 'Man allegedly tries to put wife in oven' in Chapter 3 (pages 46–7) and 'Body found in burning Castro Valley home' in Chapter 5 (pages 64–5). Study how information is reported and underline all the verbs that are used to report the information. What is the reporting verb that is used most frequently? In what tense is it used? Does it occur more frequently before or after the quote? From this activity, generalize on the use of reporting verbs in news stories.

Activity 4

Look at 'Mexico's newest icon: 22-year-old Miss Universe' in this chapter (pages 118–19). Pretend you are a journalist who has been assigned to write a very short story on the event. Write a three- to four-paragraph story, summing up or paraphrasing some of the information that is currently found in some of the quotes. You may use quotes to direct the reader's attention to any particular word/s and the reporting verbs that you know work best in the news.

Activity 5

Expressions of modality, and particularly epistemic modality are often found in economic and financial news. Look at some newspapers that deal with economics and finance – for example, the *Wall Street Journal* – or look at the business section of a national paper. Find an article that makes projections about the future economic situation of any country and observe the use of modal expressions in the text.

Further reading

Herbert, J. 2000. *Journalism in the Digital Age*, Oxford, Focal Press.

Missouri Group (B.S. Brooks, G. Kennedy, D.R. Moen and D. Ranly) 2005. *News Reporting and Writing*, 5th ed., New York, Bedford/St Martin's.

Obiedat, N. 2006. 'The pragma-ideological implications of using reported speech: the case of reporting on the Al-Aqsa intifada', *Pragmatics*, 16, 2/3, 275–304.

Palmer, F.R. 1986. *Mood and Modality*, Cambridge, Cambridge University Press.

Rich, C. 2003. *Writing and Reporting News*, Boston MA, Wadsworth/Thomson Learning.

Chapter 9

The power of words

This chapter explains how news writers can exploit the richness and expressive potential of the English language to create powerful texts and convey their slant on the topic at hand. After a description of some of the features characterizing the English vocabulary, we see how writers can use words to imply meaning, suggest irony, represent groups and establish an ideological stance.

9.1 Words as a tool for establishing an ideological stance

We have already looked at the most common ways in which bias manifests itself in the news, through the framing of a story, the sentence structure, the selection and use of sources, and the use of modal expressions. But a reader's interpretation of a news story is also influenced by the writer's conscious or unconscious choice of words used in the writing of that story. Words reveal the writer's attitudes, point of view and personality traits; they express meaning, convey semantic nuances and suggest and evoke evaluation (i.e. criticism or approval), and they can provide accurate, neutral and honest analyses of events or biased/distorted, tainted ones. This chapter looks at different ways in which words can be used in news texts to create meaning.

9.2 The expressive power of the English language

English has a huge vocabulary: *Webster's Third New International Dictionary* of the English language (published in 2002) contains 476,000 words, a number which excludes many technical and specialized terms and neologisms. No other language can boast such a rich vocabulary. The size of this vocabulary is the result of the worldwide expansion of English, first as a language of colonization and then as the language of international communication. In addition, the richness of the English vocabulary continues to be enhanced, as words acquire new shades of meaning as the language is used in novel situations. The expressive power of English is also enhanced by its great adaptability, as words, roots, affixes and prepositions can be easily combined to form new words. This makes it a very productive language and well suited to being applied to new concepts and in new situations. It is a powerful tool in the hands of writers – reporters among them.

9.2.1 Vocabulary size

The scale of the English vocabulary makes it possible to express concepts with great exactness. English has a wealth of words that are nearly **synonymous**, yet convey subtle differences of meaning. Using the appropriate word, the reporter can describe an event with detail and precision, providing different shades of meaning as appropriate to the situation. For example, the following words all describe phenomena involving light:

dazzle	glisten	flicker
shimmer	sparkle	flash
glimmer	twinkle	glow
glint	spark	

Some of the words in the list above would occur in the following possible sentences: *The candle* flickered *in the wind* (i.e., was burning or shining unsteadily); *The moonlight* shimmered *on the sea* (i.e., was shining with a wavering or soft light); *A light* glimmered *at a great distance* (i.e., had intermittent flickers or flashes of light); *A star was* glowing *in the dark* (i.e., was shining brightly); *A torch* flashed *at me in the night* (i.e., appeared briefly).

The availability of a very rich vocabulary also has some disadvantages, though. The existence of alternative, near-synonymous words makes it possible to choose a word that is *not* appropriate in a given context or for a certain style and register. For example, when referring to the place where people are physically confined for punishment, both *jail* and *prison* can be used. But these are only apparently synonyms. In the US two other words are used to refer to the type of facilities where people can be detained. The first, *penitentiary*, is a prison maintained by the federal government – it could in fact also be called a *federal prison*. The second, *correctional facility*, is a broad term for either *jail* or *prison*, which are subtypes of correctional facility; it may be used as a euphemism for all places of detention.[1] Though all four words may appear to have one and the same meaning, the choice of one term or the other in a news story would evoke semantic nuances that would not go unnoticed by many readers. Hence, it is important for reporters to choose words accurately and correctly.

English also has a wealth of near-synonymous words that differ in their level of formality, and thus are suitable for use in specific, different linguistic styles and registers. This is often true of Latinate (or Romance) words that entered the language at different times in history and were juxtaposed with Germanic words, with which they still coexist. In such cases the Latinate word is used in more formal contexts, the Germanic word in less formal ones. For example, in the list below, the words on the left are Germanic, appropriate in relatively informal registers, while those on the right are near-synonyms of Latin or Romance origin, and appropriate in relatively formal contexts (see also Chapter 7).

Germanic	**Latin/Romance**
fast	rapid
fatherly	paternal
tell	narrate
pretty	attractive
show	illustrate
talk	discuss

9.2.2 Flexibility, adaptability and borrowing

English also offers a variety of ways to form new words (neologisms) as they are needed – a process that is commonplace and provides the means to express any new idea. One way that words can be formed is by **derivation**: adding affixes (prefixes or suffixes) to a root (for example, *routinely* is derived from the root *routine* and the suffix *-ly*). Other ways are by **compounding** – combining existing words and morphemes, as with, for example, *laptop* (from *lap* + *top*) or *chairperson* (from *chair* + *person*) – or by combining words with suffixes and prepositions, as in coinages like *moviegoer* (a person who likes to go to watch movies, from *movie* + *go* + *-er*), or *fixer-upper* (meaning a house that needs substantial work doing to it, from *fix* + *er* + *up* + *-er*). In addition, new words can be created by merging together two or more existing words, so-called **blendings**. Quite a few words originally created through blendings, are now well established in English; examples are *smog* (from *smoke* + *fog*), *motel* (from *motor* + *hotel*), and *brunch* (*breakfast* + *lunch*). Words can also be created through **acronyms**, that is, when the initial portions of the words or syllables of a phrase are made to stand for the whole words, as is the case with the following words: *AIDS* = *Acquired Immune Deficiency Syndrome*; *WASP* = *White Anglo-Saxon Protestant*. Common words may originate as trademarks, brand names, etc. This is what happened to words like *xerox*, *aspirin*, *band-aid*, *kleenex*, which were originally brand names of some products and then became used to designate a type of product.

Today, a great many words are entering the English lexicon because they are widely used on the Internet. A recent acquisition of this sort is *google*. Both the online *Oxford English Dictionary Online*[2] and the

Merriam-Webster Online [American] *English Dictionary*[3] have entered this word. In the latter, the word is defined as: 'to use the Google search engine to obtain information about (as a person) on the World Wide Web'. However, it is not impossible to see that, in a near future, the meaning of the word will be extended to mean 'to look someone or something up'.

Finally, new words can enter the language through **borrowings** from other languages. In its history, English has taken words from a variety of languages spoken around the world, and has adapted them to its own uses. The list of borrowings is enormous and includes words from all kinds of semantic fields (e.g., *cannibal*, *desperado*, *ghetto*, *casino*, *umbrella*, *dollar*, *karma*, *yoga*, *jungle*, *shampoo*, *hashish*, *hurricane*, *tobacco*, *tiger*, *spaghetti*, *hamburger*, *pyjama*, *algebra*, *tea*, *nirvana*, *golf*, *ski*, *sushi*).

The easy adoption of new coinages and the capability for extensive borrowing make English a very flexible and adaptable language, with a tremendous expressive power and potential for semantic expansion.

9.3 Use of words in news reporting

Journalists' ever-changing and constantly growing vocabulary, combining foreign words, new coinages, adaptations and resemanticization, is a distinctive feature of news reporting language. It has been said that, for the sake of drawing attention, 'anything goes, no rules obtain, and everything is as good as anything else' (Laskj, 2000: 8–9). In fact, British and American newspapers make extensive use of the flexibility of the English language, and words introduced by journalists often become part of the vocabulary. Two recent coinages are *bouncebackability* and *boomerangst. Bouncebackability*, used by the *Guardian*, October 18, 2004, and quoted by the *Macmillan English Dictionary*, 2005 edition – comes from compounding *bounce* + *back* + *ability* and refers to the ability to be successful again after a period of failure. *Boomerangst* (from *boomer* + *angst*) derives from the name of a US television programme, aired by CNBC on May 14, 2008, discussing issues related to baby boomers' angst about aging in a weak job market – though the word had already been circulating for some time before that. Other more recent coinages include s*now(po)calypse* (from *snow* + *apocalypse)* and the variant forms s*nowmageddon* (from *snow* + *Armageddon*) and *snowicane* (from *snow* + *hurricane*), used as new names for winter storms since early 2009.

Neologisms are a powerful tool because they allow journalists to express concepts in novel, appealing, incisive ways, and often with fewer words (which is an extra bonus in news writing). However, creating new words in the search for conciseness may come at the expense of clarity, thus contradicting one of the basic principles of news writing itself. This is especially true of words created in connection with some event that gets wide coverage, but which later lose their aptness when the event gets forgotten. In fact, new word formations may come into vogue and then disappear as their meaning becomes progressively more opaque to the audience.

This typically happens with acronyms. For example, during the US/UK invasion of Iraq in 2003 newspapers referred to Iraq's *weapons of mass destruction* (which were sought for but not found, after being cited as the main pretext for the war itself) as *WMD* (Keeble, 2006: 95). Today this acronym would be incomprehensible to most people. On the other hand, other acronyms have survived better and become part of the language: *yuppie* (Young Urban Professional) first appeared in the *Chicago Tribune* on March 23, 1983, and has been around ever since.

The frequent use of some words, word associations or metaphors may also lead to the creation of clichés, that is, phrases or expressions that have been overused to the point of losing their intended force or novelty. Clichés are greatly disdained by news-writers, and journalists are strongly advised against using them because overexposure has so dulled their impact. A number of stock phrases seemingly continue to enjoy rude and recurrent health nonetheless, among them *tragic accident, brutal murder, sudden death, sweeping reforms, heated argument, proud parents, bare minimum, tip of the iceberg* (Keeble, 2006: 95). Like some other neologisms created by news reporters, clichés can tend to surge and then wane when they become outdated, although at times some may be adopted by a wider linguistic community and enter mainstream language.

In addition to coinages, journalists also extend existing word meaning to create new meaning. One word that has recently been used in news language with a meaning that differs from its conventional meanings is *tweet*. According to the *Merriam-Webster Online Dictionary*, the word *tweet* is a noun and is used to indicate 'a chirping note'. However, as a result of the wave of the popularity of the online social networking service Twitter, journalists started using the word *tweet* as a noun or verb to refer to messages exchanged on Twitter. These senses of the word have since been approved for use by the *Associated Press Stylebook* (issue of 06/08/2009) and entered journalists' (and audiences'?) common usage.

Finally, news reporting makes extensive use of borrowings, particularly in reports of foreign affairs, to give a 'flavour' of the language of the country where the described event takes place. For example, British newspapers often refer to foreign political figures with a word from those figures' language. In the headlines below, three European political figures are given a general title in the language of origin of the politician's countries: Angela Merkel, from Germany, is called *Frau* ('Lady' in German); Nicolas Sarkozy, from France, is called *Monsieur* ('Mister' in French); Gianfranco Fini, from Italy, is called *Signor* ('Mister' in Italian).

a) **The iron Frau: Angela Merkel**
(www.independent.co.uk, April 12, 2010)

b) **So sorry Monsieur Sarkozy, D-Day was a very BRITISH triumph**
(www.dailymail.co.uk, June 9, 2009)

c) **Signor Fini, where do you stand?**
(www.economist.com, August 5, 2010)

Like coinages, some of these borrowed words may become popular with the general public and spread into the spoken language. For example, during the 2010 Soccer World Cup, held in South Africa, the word *vuvuzuela* (a plastic trumpet blown by South African fans) became known to international audiences and enjoyed considerable popularity for some time afterwards – only to be forgotten as the months after the World Cup went by.

News services working in English around the world take advantage of the language's capability for extensive borrowing, and words from a language other than English may appear alongside English native words. This strategy, while it contributes to expanding the English vocabulary, may pose some problems for international readers of online news, who may lack the linguistic resources to fully understand the texts. The first of the two examples below uses the Hindi word *babu*, meaning bureaucrat, to refer to a senior officer under investigation and yet allowed to participate in the preparation of a white paper; the second uses the Japanese word *B-kyū gurume* to talk about the increasing popularity of some kind of Japanese-style dishes.

> **Top babu named in irrigation scam part of white paper team**
> A senior officer, whose own role in the scam is being investigated, has been allowed by the government to participate in the preparation of the white paper.
> (www.mumbaimirror.com, October 13, 2012)

> **Digging in: the rise of B-kyū gurume**
> Everyman Eats is a new column about the phenomenon of *B-kyū gurume* (B-grade gourmet) – inexpensive, down-home cooking that reflects local culinary traditions. This first instalment considers 10 moments that helped shape the recent B-kyū boom.
> (www.japantimes.co.jp, June 29, 2012)

9.4 Use of words to convey point of view

As with other linguistic strategies used in news reporting, the choice of words can reflect a particular viewpoint and influence the readership by providing an editorial comment without the reader being explicitly aware that an opinion is being conveyed. For example, using particular adjectives and adverbs in a story may reveal a hidden opinion or judgment. Thus, presenting a person as *shameless*, or a request as *hopeless*, will undoubtedly condition the readership's interpretation of the person or request referred to as being, respectively, amoral and futile.

Consider the following example, taken from a story on the traffic surge caused by the safety measures adopted for US President Obama's visit to Los Angeles, California.

Visit by President Obama causes traffic headaches in Los Angeles[4]
(www.swrnn.com, August 17, 2010)

1 Traffic jams in the West Los Angeles area caused by President Barack Obama's fundraising stop in the Southland had commuters hopping mad today, leading a City Council member to call for an investigation into ways such snarls can be avoided in the future.

2 West Los Angeles streets were congested throughout West Los Angeles Monday afternoon when Obama arrived in the city and was driven to the Beverly Hilton from Brentwood, and then later to a fundraising event in Hancock Park and back.

3 The traffic nightmares returned this morning when Obama was driven from the Beverly Hilton back to Brentwood, where he boarded a helicopter en route to Los Angeles International Airport. Heavily traveled streets near the Hilton were blocked for the bulk of the morning rush hour – forcing frustrated motorists to search for already-congested alternate routes.

4 City Councilman Bill Rosendahl plans to introduce a motion, possibly Wednesday, addressing the issue, according to spokesman Jon Fairbanks.

5 Rosendahl said he would like a report on ways the Los Angeles Police Department and city Department of Transportation can lessen traffic impacts when the president or other dignitaries visit.

6 'He (Obama) created a lot of frustration among the people who couldn't move around,' Rosendahl told ABC7. 'So we don't want to see this happen again to the president or anybody else who comes to Los Angeles.'

Through its choice of words, the article emphasizes the frustration of the local residents, suggesting a criticism of how the traffic situation was handled. This is done by using a few words that, far from being neutral, carry a negative connotation. In the headline, the tone of the article is introduced by the expression *traffic headaches* suggesting that the traffic altered the people's mood. In paragraph 1, commuters are described as *hopping mad*, and the traffic is likened to *snarls* (that is, tangles). In paragraph 3, traffic is compared to *nightmares*; the streets are described as *heavily travelled streets* and *blocked for the bulk of the morning rush hour*;

the alternate routes were *already congested*; and motorists are described as being *frustrated*. The idea of people's frustration with the traffic is repeated in paragraph 6 by quoting the words of City Councilman Rosendahl.

9.5 Irony in the news

Words can also be used to create irony, an important mechanism for establishing and reinforcing consensus between the newspaper and the readership.

Irony can be defined as the use of words to convey a meaning that is opposite to, or at odds with, their literal meaning. So, for example, an ironic statement would be to say '*What great weather we're having!*' when standing in pouring rain. Irony rests on some form of 'shared understanding' between the writer and the reader, with both recognizing that what is being communicated is not quite what is meant. In other words, irony engages the reader with different levels of meaning in a text. If the reader understands the deeper meaning intended beyond the surface meaning, then irony can lead to a pleasurable sense of satisfaction, as well as a deeper connection with the writer or the text. It is in this sense that it can be said to create consensus with the reader.

The following story is an example of using irony in a news text. The article discusses the imminent appointment of former French President Nicolas Sarkozy's son to the Presidency of the Paris business district, La Défense. This case gave rise to an uproar about nepotism in France and internationally and prompted various ironic comments from the international press. Using witty language, the author of the article portrays Sarkozy's son as an inexperienced, 23-year-old, not particularly bright undergraduate student, and his father, President Sarkozy, as a man who has little credibility in what he does or says. In so doing, the article also echoes the widespread accusations of favouring family members levelled at Sarkozy both in France and abroad.

World Agenda: 'Prince Jean' and the court of King Sarko[5]

(Charles Bremner, www.thetimes.co.uk, October 20, 2009)

1 For 10 days now, France has been witnessing a group humiliation. Cabinet ministers and presidential aides have been forced to parade in defence of the indefensible. They have had to justify the imminent elevation of Jean Sarkozy, the President's undergraduate son, to the chairmanship of La Défense, France's premier business district.

2 The promotion of 'Prince Jean', aged 23 and repeating his second year at the Sorbonne, has little impact on the administration of the land. The development chief of La Défense, the multibillion-euro island of corporate towers on the western edge of Paris, does not wield national

power. It is faintly possible that Sarko Junior could yield to the outcry and withdraw his candidacy. But whatever happens, the affair has become a defining episode for Mr Sarkozy's technicolor presidency.

3 France has talked – and joked – about little else since it learnt of the most striking act of nepotism by any recent holder of the monarchical presidency. Presidents Chirac and Mitterrand appointed their offspring to posts on their palace staff, for which they were more or less qualified. But that was nothing like the rocketing to high public office of Super Sarko's golden boy. He has no business experience and his only work so far has been 18 months as a local councillor for Neuilly, his father's fiefdom.

4 Mr Sarkozy has handed a big gift to the floundering Socialist opposition. It has been too easy for them to depict the episode as an example of how he has over-ridden the mechanisms of democracy to run everything himself. Jean's appointment flies in the face of the doctrine that took his father to power in 2007. There would be 'une rupture' – a clean break – with France's elitist ways, Mr Sarkozy promised then. Hard work and merit would be rewarded.

5 The affair has raised a question about Mr Sarkozy's famed political instinct. MPs from his own Union for a Popular Movement are wondering in private how this consummate political artist could have so blundered.

6 Mr Sarkozy has always played the outsider, and his brash cheek was a welcome change from the stuffy ways of the traditional governing class. But his pugnacious side has got the better of him this time. Rather than retreating under fire, he has attacked, depicting himself as the victim and having his people denounce the media for conducting a 'hysterical manhunt'. 'Who is the target?' he asked in *Le Figaro*. 'It is not my son. It is me. Those who have never got over my election ... are trying to attack me on all fronts with a bad faith and malice which will not deceive the French.'

7 He was wrong on that. Opinion polls show that a strong majority disapprove of the promotion of 'le fiston à piston' (the son with pull).

8 An intriguing question for the chattering classes has been how this mess was allowed to happen. *Le Monde* summed up the consensus. Mr Sarkozy has fallen victim to the 'reflexes of the court', it said. This is the phenomenon of regal insulation that has sooner or later afflicted all French presidents in the 51-year-old Fifth Republic. In other words, the courtiers do not dare tell the emperor that he is naked.

The headline introduces the two main figures of the story, that is, Jean (the son) and Nicolas Sarkozy (the father). The scene is set at a 'court' in which Jean is '*Prince Jean*' and Nicolas Sarkozy is *King Sarko*. Because neither the President nor his son are of royal blood, naming them *King* and *Prince* is a way of ridiculing them. *'Prince Jean'* is in quotes, as this is how his critics refer to him; *Sarko* is short for Sarkozy, as the President is unofficially named in France and abroad. Comparing the two Sarkozys to royal figures sets the ironical tone of the article, which – far from evoking respect for the President and his son – portrays them in a belittling manner.

The article picks up on Jean's personality and lack of talents in paragraphs 1–3, focusing on his obvious lack of academic qualities and professional experience for such a high position: *the President's undergraduate son*; *The promotion of 'Prince Jean', aged 23 and repeating his second year at the Sorbonne*; *He has no business experience and his only work so far has been 18 months as a local councillor for Neuilly*. He's implicitly described as the lucky son of a nepotistic president: *imminent elevation of Jean Sarkozy*; *the rocketing to high public office of Super Sarko's golden boy*; *his father's fiefdom*.

President Sarkozy and his actions are also described in a critical and sarcastic way: the reference to *Super Sarko* (paragraph 3) compares him to Superman, and his presidency is called *technicolor* and *monarchical*. Similarly, Neuilly is referred to as a *fiefdom* (paragraph 3). Like all kings, he is surrounded by *courtiers* (paragraph 8), and these need to fake approval: *Cabinet ministers and presidential aides have been forced to parade in defence of the indefensible* (paragraph 1); *the courtiers do not dare tell the emperor that he is naked* (paragraph 8).

The article makes extensive use of indirect speech to report and summarize the opinions of Sarkozy's critics. A few words are quoted directly, sometimes in French with a translation, to add a touch of French flavour to the news, and to make the news more vivid to the reader: *'une rupture' – a clean break* (paragraph 4); *'le fiston à piston' (the son with pull)* (paragraph 7). One speech by Sarkozy is reported in full, to personalize the character of the President and let him speak in self-defence: '*Who is the target?' 'It is not my son. It is me. Those who have never got over my election … are trying to attack me on all fronts with a bad faith and malice which will not deceive the French*' (paragraph 6). However, his words are contradicted immediately afterwards: *He was wrong on that* (paragraph 7).

Thus, through his use of words, the writer succeeds in ridiculing Sarkozy in a subtle manner, without using a harshly aggressive tone.

9.6 Representing groups in the news: a way to reinforce stereotypes and promote attitudes

Words are the basic building blocks for communicating ideas. In a text, the particular choice of words both reflects and conveys the writer's ideology and values. Because of the media's important role in today's world, the words used in the news are a powerful tool for establishing an ideological stance and promoting attitudes.

At this point a short digression on the role of news and the media in society is in order. News, like all media genres, has a major role as a source of information for people in society. This is because the discourse the media produces often functions as the foundation on which people base their conceptualization of the world. In other words, the media shapes people's knowledge, beliefs, values, opinions, social relations and identities.

An accredited social theory of discourse (e.g., Fairclough, 2001; van Dijk, 1993) views discourse in society as both a mode of representation and a mode of action. This means that media discourse both *reflects* and *constructs* the ideological system of the society in which it is produced. In other words, all linguistic choices are socially and ideologically determined, but they also contribute to creating and maintaining ideology in society. In practice, news discourse is a product of the powerful group or institution that creates it and both reflects and perpetuates the ideology of that group. Typically, the elite group that has control over the news media also benefits from being in a socially privileged position in society; the production of news is one way in which that group reproduces itself and the ideology needed to justify its privileged status in society and its continued access to social benefits.

In media discourse, strategic control of the readers' knowledge of events, and opinions about them, is crucial: it is their knowledge and opinions that influence their evaluations of events. One of the ways in which power relations are maintained is through a process of **categorization** and **dichotomization**, aimed at legitimizing the group insiders ('*Us*') and delegitimizing outsiders ('*Them*'). The dichotomy between 'Us' and 'Them' serves to polarize distinctions between 'good' and 'bad', 'victims' and 'aggressors', and to present events from particular angles. This makes it possible, for example, to de-emphasize the responsibilities of the elite group, and people who identify with them, for whatever negative events may happen and to put the blame on others. For example, terrorists are typically presented in the news with no shades of grey, and their actions are all despicable.

The process of categorization and dichotomization creates and reinforces mental schemas, which are assumed to be shared by most readers. Social **stereotypes** – simplified and rigid ideas about the specific properties and attributes implicitly associated with a social group by default – belong to this kind of social and linguistic categorization (by gender, race, social class, etc.). When social stereotypes are somehow represented or evoked in texts, it is assumed that the text will be interpreted on the basis of the readers' background knowledge of the stereotype attributes. (Jokes are a case in point: they rely on the listener/reader's implied knowledge of the stereotypes' attributes to achieve the intended humorous effect.)

Stereotypes contribute to perpetuating specific ideas about social groups, since the attributes ascribed to them are presented as the natural ones. At the same time, they reveal the ideology of the text creator. For instance, the use of the words *black* and *brown* in the next example implicitly alludes to the dominance in society of *white* children, from whom the *black* and *brown* children are set apart.

> **Villaraigosa calls for high educational standards for black, brown children**
>
> (Joy-Ann Reid, The Grio, nbclatino.com, January 21, 2013)
>
> WASHINGTON D.C. – Los Angeles Mayor Antonio Villaraigosa made an impassioned plea for addressing educational disparities among Hispanic and African-American children Sunday, saying the nation owed as much to the legacy of Rev. Martin Luther King Jr.

In the proposed division of society between *white* (implied), *black* and *brown*, the text perpetuates a division that is maintained by the white society. Note that this categorization is an oversimplification of a much more complex reality of social ethnicities, and contributes to reinforcing socially recognised mental schemas. The sub-categorization of children into *black* and *brown* is presented in a matter-of-fact way, though it has no well-defined and uncontroversial scientific basis. Finally, the fact that the news appeared in the Latino section of nbcnews.com shows that the Hispano-American minority also accepts being represented as *brown*, thus internalizing the stereotypical attribute and perpetuating the use of this word to refer to their socio-ethnic group.

Similarly, the following example presents an oversimplified categorization between *black* (or '*too black*') children and children with disabilities (or children that are '*too difficult*') as opposed, implicitly, to *white* children with no disabilities.

> **The plight of children who are last to be chosen by would-be carers**
>
> (www.walesonline.co.uk, January 22, 2013)
>
> They are the children no-one wants – 'too black' or 'too difficult' to find a foster family. Now, a campaign by Barnardo's highlights how black children and those with disabilities are left unloved in care for years.

Here too, the representation of the two groups as *black children* and *children with disabilities* defines the children by one of their attributes. In this process the children lose their individuality and are lumped together under broad categories that lose sight of their overall identity. The simplistic reduction of social groups to a single attribute – 'being black' or 'being disabled' – is a reason for discrimination or undesirability.

As these examples show, the linguistic choices made in the texts create an oversimplified and undiversified representation of the social groups that leaves no room for alternative views. This oversimplified representation of social groups in the news affects the readers' interpretation of the text in that it leads them to predict and anticipate the precise meaning that every term or linguistic element has in the text. At the same time, it helps to reinforce the perception of the reality of the group attributes.

Here are two reports of the same story that show how language can affect the representation of groups and present them in a favourable or unfavourable light.

> **Aussie classrooms reviving Aboriginal languages**
> (the *News International*, Pakistan, December 19, 2012)

> **Lost indigenous language revived in Australia**
> (Phil Mercer, BBC News, January 22, 2013)

In the first, the word used to indicate 'Australian' is *Aussie*: a word some Australians use as a term of identification for people of the traditional cultural group (of Anglo-Celtic descent). The word received international attention in 2005 in connection with an outbreak of mass racist violence initiated by white Australians against young Australian men of Middle Eastern descent.[6] In the same headline, the word used to refer to the Australian-native language is *Aboriginal*. This word, originally a synonym of 'native', was used in British colonial times to refer to the indigenous peoples of Australia. Thus, through its choice of words, the headline ironically suggests that the decision of reviving the native languages of Australia is made by the white dominant class of the country. By contrast, in the other example the news is presented in much more neutral terms: the agency has been removed from the headline, and the word used to talk about the native language is *indigenous*.

Another stereotyped category is women. It has been shown that the discourse used to talk about women in the news encodes meanings that construct them as a *special group* with specific features that set them aside from the rest of humanity. Specifically, the representation of women in the news tends to include a focus on the women's roles in their domestic lives, their relation to other people, and particularly their families, and their physical attributes or sensuality (Fowler, 1991).

Consider the following:

> **Woman thief who sedated men is jailed for five years**
> (Steven Morris, www.guardian.co.uk, January 18, 2005)
>
> A mother of two was jailed for five years yesterday after becoming the first woman to be convicted of using the drug Rohypnol to sedate male victims before stealing from them.

Paula Broadwell, biographer and mother of 2 accused of affair with David Petraeus, heaped praise on CIA director's wife

(Edgar Sandoval and Larry Mcshane, *New York Daily News*, November 10, 2012)

Neighbors are at a loss to explain how the bright, attractive West Point graduate morphed into the headline-making general's mistress.

These represent a fairly common way in which news reporting characterizes women by means of their family relationships. In both examples, the fact that the two women are *mothers of 2* is, strictly speaking, not relevant to the description of the women. However, including this attribute in the representation of the women serves a derogatory function: it conveys an implied criticism to the reader by associating negatively connoted and socially reprimandable actions, such as stealing or having an affair, and positively connoted actions, such as being a mother of two. The lead in the first example states that the woman is the *first* woman to be convicted of using the drug Rohypnol, an action that – according to the news – is typically restricted to men. The choice of the adjective *first* reinforces the implied criticism of the woman's actions, aggravating the fact that she is a mother of two doing things that women normally do not do.

The second instance implicitly lays the blame on a woman, a recognized biographer and a mother of 2, who has had an affair with a married man. The lead cites her intellectual abilities: *bright* ... *West Point graduate*; however, it also makes reference to her physical attributes, *attractive*. Finally, in describing her relationship with the CIA's director, the lead assigns her the role of *mistress*, a word that conveys the implication of 'kept woman'. Thus the article proposes a representation of the woman as someone who, in spite of being smart and professionally successful, conforms to the rather limited set of roles that women are traditionally assigned.

Here is another case of the woman in the story being associated with her physical characteristics:

German Jewish activist voted sexiest female politician

(www.jta.org, January 17, 2013)

BERLIN (JTA) – A 25-year-old Jewish woman was voted Germany's sexiest female politician.

Here the text again focuses on the woman's sexual attractiveness. It is indeed the fact that she is the *sexiest* politician that causes the story to be covered. Needless to say, this contributes to the stereotype according to which the role of 'being sexy' pertains solely to female, and not male, politicians.

9.7 Naming as a way to convey ideology

A not dissimilar way in which news texts categorize reality through word choice is by means of naming. In general, **naming** is a form of labelling, but naming people is also a way of classifying and handling social relationships. Names assign an identity, role, group membership or quality to people, and they reveal the cultural background of those who use them both to *refer* to people and to *address* them. In most cultures, naming conventions differ according to the kind of relationship that people have. For example, nicknames or first names are typically used of or among friends and family; names preceded by titles are used to show deference or respect; derogatory names are used to express dislike. In many cultures, following the wrong naming conventions when addressing people may cause insult or offense.

The following is a list of various possible ways of addressing the same person, from more formal and distanced, to less formal and more affectionate.

Dr Robertson	Charlie
Mr Robertson	Buddy
Sir	Honey
Charles	Dad
Robertson	Dumbhead

Of the modes of address in the left-hand column, *Dr Robertson* is likely to be used by a patient or by someone who recognizes the doctor as having higher social status or education than they have (for example, a nurse, a student); *Mr Robertson* would probably be used in a formal encounter by a person who does not know Robertson's job; *Sir* would typically be used by a stranger to address him in a restaurant, on the street, etc.; *Charles* would be used by an acquaintance. Finally, using the single last name *Robertson* as an address form would signify that the speaker is, or feels he is, of superior status to the addressee. Of the terms in the right column, *Charlie* would be the form used by a friend, and *Buddy* by a former schoolmate, or a sports friend. Finally, *Honey* would be used by Robertson's wife, and *Dad* by his child; *Dumbhead* would be used in a derogatory manner by a critic of his, or (ironically) by a friend. But even apparently neutral or nice-sounding terms can become derogatory if used inappropriately, in the wrong context. For example, if a fellow doctor addressed Robertson with the endearment term *Honey* in a sarcastic tone, that would be interpreted as a way to diminish or obscure Robertson's professional role.

Thus, *President Obama*, *Barack Obama*, and *Barack* are all possible ways of naming the President of the US. However, while *President Obama* is the expected convention in news texts, a story that refers to him as *Barack* may do so to indicate comradeship or affection – or, alternatively, to convey a sense of superiority, a lack of deference, or dislike.

In written texts, the system of naming can be used to convey and impose point of view on the reported event. For example, in accounts of the events preceding the opening of the G20 summit on April 1, 2009, the people in conflict with the police were called: *demonstrators*, *protesters* or *rioters*.

G20 demonstrators march in London

(www.bbc.co.uk, March 28, 2009)

G20 protesters clash with London cops

(www.cbsnews.com, April 1, 2009)

G20 protests: rioters loot RBS as demonstrations turn violent

(www.telegraph.co.uk, April 1, 2009)

The three words represent different ways of referring to the group of people in the report: while *demonstrators* is the most neutral word, *protesters* is somewhat negative, and *rioters* is definitely negative and judgmental. So the words are not equivalent: they may denote the same group of people, but they convey different connotations about them.

The naming strategies adopted in a text can thus impart ideology, each term choice giving a different slant to the description of the people being referred to. In a novel, the characters' names sometimes reflect some of their qualities. For example, a protagonist called *Bella* will evoke the idea that she is beautiful, and the character in Disney's film *101 Dalmatians* is called *Cruella de Vil* to suggest that she is an evil person. In the news, too, the naming strategy used to describe or talk about a person will have an effect on the readers' opinion of that person.

This is exemplified in the articles below, all of which report the same story. That story is about a man, Levi Bellfield, who was found guilty of killing two young women and attempting to kill another. At the time of his conviction he was also the main suspect in the killing of another young woman, Milly Dowler, and was linked to the homicide of 20 women, all of them young (from 13 to 37), slim, blonde and well-off. The story received a great deal of attention, not only because of the brutality of the killings (he would kill women with a hammer), but also because it was claimed that mistakes had been made in the police investigations, with the result that the man remained free and able to kill for many years before he was eventually uncovered. All UK national papers covered the story and interpreted the audience's opinion by evincing compassion for the young women and presenting the man in a negative light. However, they differed in the amount of coverage they gave to the story, as well as in the types of judgment they transmitted to the reader through the choice of words used to present the facts, the victim and the killer.

Violent woman-hater is main Milly Dowler murder suspect[7]

(*The Times*, February 26, 2008)

1 The man convicted yesterday of murdering two women and trying to kill a third was left free to continue his campaign of violence against women because of basic investigative errors by police.

2 Levi Bellfield was found guilty at the Old Bailey of murdering Marsha McDonnell, 19, and Amelie Delagrange, 22, and attempting to murder Kate Sheedy. He was then identified as the prime suspect for the unresolved murder of the schoolgirl Milly Dowler.

3 A Scotland Yard task force has been set up to investigate Bellfield's possible connection to a series of 20 murders, attempted murders and other attacks dating back 25 years.

4 Detective Chief Inspector Colin Sutton said that Bellfield was a dangerous man and that women would be safer now that he was behind bars. He stalked his victims, all young and blonde, as they waited for – or stepped off – buses late at night.

5 Police said that they expected more victims of Bellfield, 39, a wheel clamper, to come forward after his picture was widely published for the first time.

6 As officers promised to uncover the full extent of Bellfield's crimes, it became clear that vital clues were missed which could have led to his arrest two years before he was eventually detained.

7 Four officers from the Metropolitan Police have been reprimanded for serious errors in the inquiry into the attempted murder of Kate Sheedy in Isleworth in May 2004, three months before Miss Delagrange's death.

8 Bellfield attacked Miss Sheedy, now 21, with his car, knocking her down then driving over her twice.

In *The Times* the news is covered on pages 22–3 (See page 22 in Figure 9.1). The article presents all the facts relating to the various murders which Bellfield was suspected of committing, and explains why Bellfield was allowed to go free two years before he was eventually detained. In the headline Bellfield is introduced as a *violent woman-hater* and *main murder suspect*. The expression *main murder suspect* introduces the man in terms of his probable – rather than certain – implication in the crime as well as suspending judgment on him until he has been tried for this murder (the word *main* implies that there may be other suspects as well; and the word *suspect* does not indicate that the man *is* the culprit). In the body copy, Bellfield is called *the man* (paragraph 1), *Levi Bellfield* (paragraph 2), or *Bellfield* (paragraphs 3–6). The article also introduces Bellfield's job, when it says he was a *wheel clamper* (paragraph 5) – that is, someone licensed to immobilize the wheels of vehicles illegally parked in car parks or on public streets. Overall, the article tries to avoid referring to Bellfield by names that could express judgment (with the exception of *violent woman-hater* in the headline). As for the victims, they are called by their first and last names – *Milly Dowler* (headline and paragraph 2), *Marsha McDonnell* and *Amelie Delagrange* (paragraph 2) – that is, using neutral, non-emotional language. In most of the paragraphs Bellfield is made the subject of passive constructions (*the man convicted ... was left free*; *was found guilty*; *was identified*; *his picture was widely published*; *he was eventually detained*) or relational verbs (*violent woman-hater is main murder suspect*; *Bellfield was a dangerous man*; *he was behind bars*), and his responsibility in the murders is attenuated (*Bellfield's possible connection to a series of 20 murders*). His direct responsibility in the crimes is cited only twice in the first eight paragraphs (*he stalked his victims*; *Bellfield attacked Miss Sheedy*). Overall, *The Times* does not want to minimize Bellfield's guilt in the crimes for which he is accused, but refrains from openly expressing judgment, as the man has not yet been found guilty.

A different representation of the 'same' facts is provided by the story published in the *Daily Telegraph* on the same day.

> **Bus stop killer's link to Milly**[8]
> Nightclub bouncer who murdered two young women is prime suspect in schoolgirl's death
>
> (the *Daily Telegraph*, February 26, 2008)

1 A former nightclub bouncer was named yesterday as the prime suspect in the killing of the schoolgirl Milly Dowler after being found guilty of a murderous campaign against women.

2 Levi Bellfield was once convicted at the Old Bailey of the 'hammer murders' of the students Marsha McDonnell, 19, and Amelie Delagrange, 22, as well as the attempted murder of a schoolgirl, Kate Sheedy.

3 But at the conclusion of his trial, it emerged that Bellfield stalked the streets of affluent suburbs for two decades targeting lone women and girls – and is thought to be responsible for up to 20 other attacks.

4 The disclosure led last night to questions over how police had taken so long to realise that a serial attacker – the Bus Stop Killer – was on the loose.

5 Detectives will now question Bellfield over 'compelling' evidence allegedly linking him to the unsolved killing of Amanda Dowler, known as Milly, in Walton-on-Thames, Surrey, almost six years ago. The 13-year-old disappeared on her way home from school in March 2002 and detectives believe that there are up to 10 pieces of circumstantial evidence to link him to the abduction and murder.

6 When Milly disappeared, Bellfield was staying only a short distance from the road where she was last seen. He had access to a red car, similar to the one caught on CCTV at the time she was abducted.

The *Daily Telegraph*, which dedicated the whole front page to the story, draws the readers' attention by calling Bellfield the *bus stop killer* and Milly Dowler simply *Milly*. Introducing Bellfield as a *killer*, the headline conveys a negative judgment of him. In the subhead, Bellfield, who is named by his night job title (*nightclub bouncer*), is the subject of the active verb *murdered*, which makes him directly responsible for the action of murdering. The subhead also says that Bellfield is the *prime suspect* in Milly Dowler's death. The victim is called by her first name only, *Milly*, to introduce her as a person who could be close to the reader, like a friend or a daughter, and reinforce the readers' sympathy for the young victim.

In the story Bellfield is described as *a former nightclub bouncer* (paragraph 1), and then as *Levi Bellfield* (paragraph 2), or *Bellfield* (paragraphs 3 and 5). He is also referred to as *a serial attacker – the Bus stop Killer*, in paragraph 4. As for the victims, they are referred by first and last names (*Marsha McDonnell*; *Amelie Delagrange*; *Kate Sheedy*). Milly Dowler is first introduced by first and last name (paragraphs 1, 5) and then simply called *Milly* (paragraphs 5, 6). Milly is also described as being a *schoolgirl* (subhead), and *a 13-year-old* (paragraph 5). Bellfield is made the subject of passive constructions (*was named*; *after being found*; *was convicted*; *is thought to be responsible*), as well as relational verbs (*the Bus Stop Killer was on the loose*; *had access*), and action verbs (*Bellfield stalked the streets*; *was staying*).

While this article presents the events and the people involved in an apparently objective manner, the bias is hidden in the emphasis on the contrast between Bellfield, the killer, on the one side, and the young schoolgirl Milly on the other.

The *Sun* provides yet a different account of the events through different naming choices. The story that appeared on the paper's front page is shown below (see also Figure 9.2).

Bus Stop Beast Found Guilty[9]
HE KILLED MILLY TOO
Now Dowler cops believe maniac Levi Bellfield murdered schoolgirl
(the *Sun*, February 26, 2008)

1 A monster convicted yesterday of bludgeoning two girls to death at random also murdered Milly Dowler, cops feared last night.

2 Bus stop beast Levi Bellfield, 39 – who armed himself with a hammer to hunt for prey – slaughtered Marsha McDonnell, 19, and French student Amelie Delagrange, 22, simply because he hated slim young blondes.

3 Last night the 20st muscleman was named prime suspect in the 2002 murder of 13-year-old Milly as cops planning to grill him relaunched the case that horrified Britain.

The *Sun* also dedicates the whole front page to the story. As is typical of tabloids, the news is presented with no shades of grey, to create a high emotional impact on the reader. Bellfield is introduced as a *bus stop beast* (headline and paragraph 2), a *maniac* (subhead), *a monster* (paragraph 1), or otherwise as a man 'physically fit' for murder*: the 20st muscleman* (paragraph 3). He is also described as guilty: *bus stop beast found guilty* (banner headline) – although, in fact, he had been found guilty of previous murders, but not of murdering Milly Dowler (it was only later that he was convicted of that). In the headline, Bellfield is introduced with the pronoun *he* in the sentence *He killed Milly too*, implying that he is well-known to readers for his murders and suggesting that he is responsible for yet another crime. Only in paragraph 3 does the reader find out that Bellfield is only *a prime suspect* in the Dowler case. All in all – through the combination of word choice, missing specifications and the order of presentation of the reported events – readers might be led to assume that Bellfield is responsible for murdering Milly Dowler.

Syntactically, Bellfield is made the subject of a number of action verbs, mostly used to describe his crude, violent actions: he *killed Milly* (headline); *murdered schoolgirl* (subhead); *armed himself with a hammer to hunt for prey* (paragraph 2); *slaughtered Marsha McDonnell* (paragraph 2). He is also the subject of two passive constructions: *A monster convicted* (paragraph 1); *the 20st muscleman was named* (paragraph 3). This allows the recurrent thematization of subjects having the same referent (i.e., Levi Bellfield), and creates a logical link in the three paragraphs of the story focusing on the brutality of the man (*A monster... Bus stop beast... the 20st muscleman...*).

The brutality of the man is contrasted with the figure of the young victim, referred to with the endearing nickname *Milly* (headline and paragraph 3), with the word *schoolgirl* (subhead), or as Milly Dowler (paragraph 1).

In sum, the three stories show how adopting different naming strategies can directly affect the ideological slant of texts: while none of the texts shows favour to Bellfield, *The Times* provides the most balanced account of the events, by refraining from expressing an explicit opinion on the suspect; the *Daily Telegraph* implies that Bellfield is guilty of the murders for which he is the prime suspect and yet gives data to provide an accurate report of the event; the *Sun* describes Bellfield in terms that might lead readers to assume his guilt, even though he has not yet been tried for the Dowler murder. The contrast between the perspective on the man given by *The Times* and the *Sun* is reinforced in the visual appearance of the two texts. *The Times* focuses on showing objective data relating to the story; in the *Sun* the image of a man 'physically fit' for murder is reinforced by the front-page picture showing Bellfield in a *muscleman* pose.

As the above discussion has shown, the newspaper slant on a particular event conditions both the text and its visual presentation.

22 | News

Levi Bellfield

Violent woman-hater is main Milly Dowler murder suspect

▶ Police errors left killer free to continue attacks

▶ Task force to examine links to 20 other cases

Victims

Figure 9.1 Page 22 of *The Times* of February 26, 2008, reporting on Levi Bellfield.[10]

THE Sun 20p

TWO FREE TICKETS TO Alton Towers

WORTH £68

TOKEN: PAGE 22

BUS STOP BEAST FOUND GUILTY

HE KILLED MILLY TOO

Now Dowler cops believe maniac Levi Bellfield murdered schoolgirl

Figure 9.2 Front page of the *Sun* of February 26, 2008, reporting on Levi Bellfield.[11]

Students' activities

Activity 1

Look at the list of words below. Using your dictionary, find for each word in the left-hand column a Germanic synonym (e.g.: *absurdity* – *foolishness*; *acquire* – *get*).

Latin/French Origin	Germanic
absurdity	foolishness
acquire	get
apprehend	
attempt	
construct	
depart	
exacerbate	
legislation	
necessity	
senile	
stupefy	
spectacular	

Activity 2

In a paper you believe to express strong opinions, look for articles that you think are sexist, racist or prejudiced. Look at how language is used in those stories. Consider naming, the use of adjectives, choice of verbs, etc.

Activity 3

Read the story in Chapter 5, section 5.5, and analyse how Rebecca Cain and Wilfred Museka are represented. In particular, look at the amount and type of information provided about each individual and the number and type of adjectives used to refer to the two individuals and/or their actions. Reflect on whether this story creates and reinforces a possible anti-immigrant feeling in the readership.

Activity 4

Section 9.5 of this chapter provided a definition of irony as involving an incongruity between the literal and the implied meanings of words. However, irony may not be easy to recognize in a text.

For this activity, take the text 'Suspicious wives master the art of high-tech spying' on pages 89–90 and study it to see where you find examples of irony.

Clue: A possible way to convey irony is by using pompous language for things of little relevance, and vice versa.

Activity 5

The headlines below were used in different newspapers on June 26, 2009 to head stories reporting the death of the famous pop singer Michael Jackson. The naming strategies used in the different papers assume and promote different responses from their audiences. In particular, the way they refer to Jackson implies a certain kind of relationship of the audience with the singer. For example, the use of informal or slang expressions signals intimacy; on the contrary the use of formal language signals distance. Also, the use of particular names indicates role recognition.

By looking at these headlines, what kind of relationship do you think is assumed and how does the particular name chosen to refer to Jackson indicate that?

'King of pop' dies	(the *Anniston Star*)
Michael Jackson dies	(*Daily Times*)
The King of Pop is gone	(the *Bakersfield California*)
Michael Jackson, pop's uneasy king, dead at 50	(the *Boston Globe*)
Music loses icon	(*Press Telegram*)
'We have lost an icon'	(the *Indianapolis Star*)
Gone too soon	(the *Gleaner*)
Fade to Blacko	(the *Boston Herald*)

Further reading

Associated Press Inc., 2009. *Associated Press Stylebook and Briefing on Media Law*, New York, Basic Books.

Denning, K., Kessler, B., and Leben, W.R. 2007. *English Vocabulary Elements*, New York, Oxford University Press.

Katsiavriades, K. 1997, 2002. 'The origin and history of the English language', www.krysstal.com/english.html.

Kemmer, S. 2011. 'Loanwords: Major periods of borrowing in the history of English', www.ruf.rice.edu/~kemmer/Words/loanwords.html.

Merriam-Webster OnLine. www.merriam-webster.com/, Chicago IL, Encyclopædia Britannica.

Oxford English Dictionary Online. 2012. oxforddictionaries.com/, Oxford, Oxford University Press.

Pape, S., and Featherstone, S. 2005. *Newspaper Journalism: A Practical Introduction*, London, Sage.

Pennebaker, J.W. 2011. *The Secret Life of Pronouns: What Our Words Say About Us*, New York, Bloomsbury.

Shapiro, F.R. 1986. 'Yuppies, yumpies, yaps, and computer-assisted lexicology', *American Speech*, 61, 2, 139–46.
van Dijk, T.A. 1995. 'Power and the news media', in D. Paletz (ed.), *Political Communication and Action*, Cresskill NJ, Hampton Press, 9–36.
Webster's Third New International Dictionary, 2002, Springfield MA, Merriam Webster.

Epilogue

We have reached the end of this introduction to the language of the news. While there is more to learn about the subject, this is a good point to stop, to summarize, and to look ahead.

News plays a vital role in human affairs. It keeps us informed of what is happening in our own country and in the world at large. Its importance has been greatly increased by the spread of education, which sharpens and cultivates our curiosity about what happens around us. In addition, technology has metaphorically shortened the distance to the different corners of the world, turning us into citizens of the globe. All this has increased our need to be informed about the world we live in.

In the last ten years, major changes have affected news delivery and consumption. Ten years ago the Internet was in its infancy, and most people got their news from newspapers, the television and the radio. Today, though, more and more people turn to the Internet for news, and, with the Internet becoming more and more widespread, accessible, fast and reliable, people can be connected and stay online at all times. Staying connected 24/7 is becoming the norm and the most important factor in the growth of web-based application use.

The advent of the Internet, and the opportunity to stay informed around the clock have changed the relationship between the newsreader and the news provider. Before the Internet, the public and the journalists were accustomed to a 24-hour news cycle, but today people expect to see eye-witness accounts of events as they are occurring.

This has affected the whole process of news production and journalists' practices of news gathering and reporting. Newspapers face fierce competition from news provided via the Internet by online service providers, press releases and social media. To fight for readers' attention, journalists have to provide content in a form that responds to the changing consumers' needs. Increasingly, they are having to learn to multi-skill, produce stories for multiple formats and incorporate more images, audios and videos in their stories.

Blogs and social media are being used as tools for news-gathering and dissemination, for investigation and crowd-sourced fact checking. The conversations that take place in social media influence the news that gets reported. Thus, social networks are becoming the filters, curators and distribution channels for news, and consumers are active in the news-gathering and distribution process.

The continuous evolution and adaptation of technology and information systems, the backbone of the news production process, leads to rapid changes in the way news is structured and delivered today. Many of the formats currently used to deliver news through the Internet or with web-based applications may be transient, and in a few years may take different forms.

On the other hand, some of the features that characterize news writing still form the basis for reporting stories. Journalists learn news-writing skills as part of their profession and use them for experimenting when new formats come along. Some basic linguistic tools that allow writers to present information from a particular angle are widely used in both print and online journalism.

This book has discussed how, consciously or unconsciously, journalists may promote different interpretations of the news through the linguistic choices they make in their texts. Knowing how language is used in the text can help the reader understand how the message is construed and 'read through' the news.

I hope that readers will use this recipe whenever they read news, in whatever format.

Notes

Introduction

1 Adapted from www.clusterconvention.org/files/2012/06/Opening_Statement_FODSA-CMC.pdf.

1 Making news

1 These terms are explained in Chapter 4, section 4.5.
2 All the examples in this activity are invented, though they were created on the basis of real stories.

2 Defining news

1 Copyright of the Independent News and Media Limited, London, UK. Used with permission.
2 Copyright of the *China Daily*, China. Used with permission.
3 Copyright of Al Nisr Publishing LLC, Dubai, UAE. Used with permission.
4 Copyright of the *Global Times*, Beijing, China. Used with permission.
5 *Dancheong* refers to Korean traditional decorative colouring on wooden buildings and artefacts.
6 Objectivity is required in so-called 'hard news' (see section 2.4), but is obviously not required in editorials, political columns, or art and movie critical reviews, where journalists are purposely required to express their opinions.
7 Copyright of the Boston Herald Incorporation, USA. Used with permission.
8 Copyright of Daily News, L.P., New York, USA. Used with permission.

3 Sourcing news

1 Copyright of the *China Daily*, China. Used with permission.
2 Copyright of www.msnbc.msn.com/. Used with permission.
3 See Chapter 7 for a more detailed explanation.
4 Used with permission of the Associated Press Copyright © 2012. All rights reserved.

4 Conveying meaning through design

1 Copyright of the Telegraph Media Group Limited 2008/2012, UK. Used with permission.

2 Copyright of Guardian News and Media Limited 2012, UK. Used with permission.
3 Copyright of Trinity Mirror Group, UK. Used with permission.
4 Copyright of the Boston Herald Incorporation, USA. Used with permission.
5 A pica is a typographic unit of measurement corresponding to 1⁄6th of an inch. It is subdivided into 12 units called points.

5 Structuring the story

1 www.nmauk.co.uk/nma/do/live/research?researchModel=1143.
2 Copyright of *San Francisco Chronicle*, USA. Used with permission.
3 Copyright of Reading Eagle Company, USA. Used with permission.
4 Copyright of the Washington Post News Media Services. Used with permission.
5 Due to copyright constraints, the original image could not be included here, but it can be found at: www.express.co.uk/posts/view/346593/Crash-victim-an-aspiring-model.
6 Copyright of Press Association, UK. Used with permission.
7 Copyright of News International Trading Ltd. Used with permission.

6 Headline, lead and story proper

1 A more comprehensive account of nominalization is given in Chapter 7.
2 www.phrases.org.uk/meanings/65500.html.
3 For example, this headline also appeared in the following newspapers from the UK: the *Independent*, on December 16, 1997 ('Weather: From Russia with gloves' – where the word *gloves* is associated with 'cold'); the *Sunday Sun* of March 13, 2004 ('From Russia with gloves'); the www.bbc.co.uk online news service of July 6, 2005 ('From Russia with gloves'); the www.mirror.co.uk edition of May 22, 2008 ('From Russia with gloves: Goalie clinches win for Manchester United', where the word *gloves* refers to the gloves of the goalkeeper of the Manchester United soccer team).
4 Copyright of *Daily Mail*, the *Mail on Sunday* and Metro Media Group. Used with permission.
5 Copyright of News International Trading Ltd. Used with permission.

7 The tools of the trade

1 Copyright of News International Trading Ltd. Used with permission.
2 Copyright of *Daily Mail*, the *Mail on Sunday* and Metro Media Group. Used with permission.
3 Copyright of *Los Angeles Times*, Tribune Company. Used with permission.

8 Reporting information and evaluating likelihood

1 Used with permission of the Associated Press Copyright © 2012. All rights reserved.
2 Copyright of Daily News, L.P., New York, USA. Used with permission.
3 Copyright of Yonhap News Agency, Seoul, South Korea. Used with permission.

9 The power of words

1. The definitions of these terms are adapted from the *Merriam-Webster Online Dictionary* at: www.merriam-webster.com.
2. oxforddictionaries.com.
3. www.merriam-webster.com.
4. Used with permission of Southwest Riverside News Network Copyright © 2013. All Rights Reserved.
5. Copyright of News International Trading Ltd. Used with permission.
6. en.wikipedia.org/wiki/Aussie.
7. Copyright of News International Trading Ltd. Used with permission.
8. Copyright of the Telegraph Media Group Limited 2008/2012, UK. Used with permission.
9. Copyright of News International Trading Ltd. Used with permission.
10. Copyright of News International Trading Ltd. Used with permission.
11. Copyright of News International Trading Ltd. Used with permission.

References

Campbell, V. 2004. *Information Age Journalism: Journalism in an International Context*, London, Arnold.

Conboy, M. 2007. *The Language of the News*, London and New York, Routledge.

Fairclough, N. 2001. *Language and Power*, Harlow, Longman.

Fowler, R. 1991. *Language in the News: Discourse and Ideology in the Press*, London, Routledge.

House of Lords Select Committee on Communication, 2008. *The Ownership of the News. Volume I: Report*, London, Stationery Office.

Ihlström, C., and Lundberg, J. 2003. 'The online news genre through the user perspective', *Proceedings of 36th Hawaii International Conference on Systems Science, Hawaii*, csdl.computer.org/comp/proceedings/hicss/2003/1874/04/18744 0103a.pdf.

Itule, B.D., and Anderson, D.A. 2007. *News Writing and Reporting*, Boston MA, McGraw Hill.

Keeble, R. 2006. *The Newspapers Handbook*, 4th edn, London and New York, Routledge.

Labov, W. 1997. 'Some further steps in narrative analysis', *Journal of Narrative and Life History*, 7, 395–415.

Labov, W., and Waletzky, J. 1967. 'Narrative analysis: oral versions of personal experience', in J. Holm (ed.), *Essays on the Verbal and Visual Arts*, Seattle, University of Washington Press, 12–44.

Lansen, J., and Stephens, M. 2008. *Writing and Reporting the News*, 3rd ed., Oxford and New York, Oxford University Press.

Laskj, M.J. 2000. *The Language of Journalism*, Volume One: *Newspaper Culture*, New Brunswick NJ, Transaction Publishers.

McAdams, M. 1995. 'Inventing an online newspaper', *Interpersonal Computing and Technology: An Electronic Journal for the 21st Century*, 3, 3, 64–90.

Pape, S., and Featherstone, S. 2005. *Newspaper Journalism: A Practical Introduction*, London, Sage.

Rich, C. 2003. *Writing and Reporting News*, Belmont CA, Wadsworth/Thomson Learning.

Rundell, M. 2005. *Macmillan English Dictionary: For Advanced Learners of American English*, Basingstoke, Palgrave Macmillan.

van Dijk, T. A. 1993. 'Principles of critical discourse analysis', *Discourse and Society*, 4, 249–83.

Wilkinson, J. 2003. 'What is media convergence? Different ideas about technology and media', *Media Digest*, Hong Kong, RTHK, www.rthk.org.hk/mediadigest/200304.html.

Index

Please note that only examples for which there is significant discussion have been included in the index.

Page numbers in italics refer to figures and bold to student activities.

The entry for the 2012 Olympic Games closing ceremony appears in the index before alphabetic entries.